The Secrets of Starting a Business

A Handbook

Philip Doggett FCMA FCGMA FIC CMC FRSA

Lamplight Research and Writing
10 Arnold Close
Stoke Mandeville
Aylesbury, Bucks HP22 5XZ

ISBN 978-1-5272-5813-6

June 2020

For Alison, Laura, Simon, Gail, Billy, Eddie and Charlie

Acknowledgements

I would like to deeply thank all my many clients over the years, the colleagues I had the privilege to work with, and my family for supporting me through a career running my own business.

Special thanks go to the very select band of proof-readers who helped focus the book and confirmed my overall approach, including my wife Alison, Allan Niblo of Vertigo Films, Ian Mackey of Buckinghamshire Business First, my daughter Laura, my son Simon, and my daughter-in-law Gail.

Thanks also go to Dr Jon Wardle and the National Film and Television School, and to my Editor who remains nameless, but taught me a lot about my 'Known Unknowns' of punctuation and the English language. Thanks also go to the Imperial War Museum, for their help and permission to reproduce the image on page 226.

Philip Doggett

June 2020

Table of Contents

Acknowledgements 4

Introduction 9

Part 1 – What is running a business all about? 13

Chapter 1 Businesses in the UK – a background 13

Chapter 2 Survival of the fittest – the evolution of success 16

Chapter 3 Competition 20

Chapter 4 Gaining 'The Knowledge' and understanding how to run a business quickly 22

Chapter 5 What do you know about running a business? 25

Chapter 6 The stages of starting a new business 28

Part 2 – Are you suited to running your own business? ... 32

Chapter 7 What is an 'entrepreneur'? 32

Chapter 8 What are the characteristics of a successful entrepreneur? 35

Chapter 9 Personal skill sets and stocktake 38

Chapter 10 'Propose Solutions Not Problems' 43

Chapter 11 The downsides – why running a business is challenging 46

Chapter 12 The upside – why running a business is fantastic 55

Part 3 – Starting a business – what is the mission? 59

Chapter 13 What are the 'Six Questions' that need to be asked? 59

Chapter 14 The mission statement 64

Chapter 15 Which business model will you use – 'traditional' or 'disrupt'? 67
Chapter 16 Research, research and research 72
Chapter 17 Barriers to entry 79
Chapter 18 Working capital 82
Chapter 19 Ethics 85
Chapter 20 Help and assistance – mentoring and non-executive directors 88
Part 4 – Starting a business – planning the mission 93
Chapter 21 A final mission plan, budget and cash flow ... 93
Chapter 22 Unique selling points (USPs) 99
Chapter 23 SWOT analysis 103
Chapter 24 Internet and social media 107
Chapter 25 Location and co-operative working spaces .. 111
Chapter 26 Intellectual property 115
Chapter 27 Teams and partners 120
Part 5 – Starting a business – on the launchpad 124
Chapter 28 Legal, tax, and commercial aspects 124
Chapter 29 Ownership of the business – key percentages of voting shares 132
Chapter 30 How to win at finance 135
Chapter 31 How much should I charge? 143
Chapter 32 How do I work out my costs? 149
Chapter 33 Optimising the transition and making the leap 154
Part 6 – Launch – 'We have ignition' 158
Chapter 34 Creating the winning mindset 158

Chapter 35 How do I win business? 161

Chapter 36 The front office – marketing and selling 173

Chapter 37 Negotiating the deals 182

Chapter 38 Back office: Scorekeeping and administration 186

Part 7 – Cash and costs 192

Chapter 39 Cash is king 192

Chapter 40 Keeping costs down 202

Part 8 – Survival and growth 204

Chapter 41 Support groups 204

Chapter 42 What could possibly go wrong? 206

Chapter 43 Lessons from the greatest entrepreneur ever? 209

Chapter 44 Staying in business: important things to remember 212

Part 9 – Coronavirus COVID-19 and their impacts 214

Chapter 45 Coronavirus: what has happened? 214

Chapter 46 Coronavirus: consequences and risks 216

Chapter 47 Coronavirus: opportunities and rewards 219

Chapter 48 Coronavirus: a winning mindset 225

Chapter 49 Coronavirus: major long-term changes 228

Chapter 50 Cash is no longer king – it is almighty 232

Appendix 1 The '50 secrets of starting a business' 235

Appendix 2 The 11-item post-Coronavirus business start-up checklist 241

Appendix 3: The 10 key things to manage day-to-day 242

Appendix 4: The seven key skills 243

Appendix 5: The 'Six Questions' that need to be clearly answered in the business plan 244

Index 245

Introduction

Apollo 11

Last year, in July 2019, the 50th anniversary of the Moon landings took place. In May 1961, President Kennedy set the mission to go to the Moon. Just over eight years later, the Apollo 11 Project put men on the Moon on 20th July 1969. It safely returned them to Earth on 24th July 1969. The Apollo Programme employed 400,000 people and put 12 people on the Moon over an 8-year period.

I have used Apollo 11 as an analogy and a theme for this book, as the successful 8-year project covers much of the same ground as starting a new business:

- Having a clear, unambiguous mission
- Doing something that has not been done before
- High risk and danger (financial)
- A highly competitive situation (USA vs. USSR)
- Having a great team
- Much research, and learning by trial and error
- A steep learning curve
- Improvised lifesaving solutions
- Successful delivery
- The need to develop new solutions
- A successful outcome

Coronavirus COVID-19

This book was started before the Coronavirus became a worldwide issue. The virus, and its impact on business generally has made starting a new business more challenging but has also opened up several major opportunities for new businesses. There is more about the impact of the Coronavirus in Part 9, Chapters 45 to 50.

Brexit

The outcome of Brexit, its impact and its resolution is another unknown, where opportunities may open up. Existing businesses are forced to deal with the changes as they arise, and some business sectors may become more challenging. New businesses starting out should have a clear view of the impacts of Brexit on their markets and associated regulation included in their business plans at the outset.

The legal part

The book is aimed at people considering starting their own business. It may also be a useful resource for new or established entrepreneurs, and also people considering or starting a portfolio career.

This book is based on my personal experiences over a thirty-five-year career running my own business, having a portfolio career, and mentoring business start-ups in the UK.

I have run or worked with (or for) nearly all the types of UK business as owner, management consultant, mentor, finance director, and troubleshooter:

- Self-Employment
- Partnership
- Umbrella Company
- Private Limited Company
- UK Public Limited Company
- Company Limited by Guarantee
- UK Charity

Author work experience types of UK business

	Shareholder or Owner	Employee	Interim or Consultant
Self Employment	Yes		Yes
Partnership	Yes		
Umbrella Company		Yes	
Private Limited Company	Yes	Yes	Yes
UK Public Limited Company	Yes	Yes	Yes
Company Limited by Guarantee	Yes		Yes
UK Charity			Yes

I have been involved in many business start-ups, including several venture capital-backed businesses, and have mentored start-ups over many years with The Prince's Trust, the National Film and Television School and more recently with Buckinghamshire Business First.

This book will not necessarily cover every type of business, but is helpful, particularly to sole traders, the self-employed, and those setting up new private limited companies.

Readers' circumstances, industries, sectors and experience will be very different, but I hope that the lessons I have learned along the way may help others with their business journey and success.

Running a new business is a complex subject, and I have aimed to provide useful practical experience and information in one place, hoping that it may prove valuable to readers.

Gender and diversity

This book has been written for everybody. I am a great believer in equal opportunities for all people, regardless of gender, ethnicity, age, sexual orientation, disability or access to higher education. Where genders are used (e.g. 'he') all genders are implied.

Further research will be needed

The book seeks to cover, in detail, the complex interactions and elements affecting a new business. It highlights those factors required to be addressed to succeed. There will be areas which require further research by readers, particularly those time-sensitive subjects which change quickly, such as tax and legislation, and government support.

This book reveals the:

- **The '50 secrets of starting a business', with clear 'Next actions'**
- **The '11-item post-Coronavirus start-up checklist'**
- **The '10 key things to manage day-to-day'**
- **The '7 key skills' needed to run a business**
- **The '6 questions' that need to be clearly answered in the business plan**

Disclaimer

All the views expressed in this book are my opinions and they are 'not to be relied upon'. They simply demonstrate what has worked or not worked for me, my mentees or clients. No liability of any kind is accepted, implied or given.

Part 1 – What is running a business all about?

Chapter 1 Businesses in the UK – a background

A nation of shopkeepers

The UK has a long history of business and entrepreneurship. Long ago, in 1794 after the Napoleonic Wars, the French made the accusation that we were 'a nation of shopkeepers'. That trend has accelerated to the present day, with the rapid rise of self-employment and a booming gig economy.

What is the 'gig economy'?

The gig economy is a free market system in which temporary positions are common and organisations contract with independent workers for short-term engagements. The term "gig" is a slang word meaning "a job for a specified period of time" and is typically used in referring to musicians. (whatis.com)

Rapid change in the last forty years

The gig economy has always been around, with people doing work if they had talent and there was a market for their services or goods. I worked early in the gig economy starting in 1970 as a jazz musician doing 'gigs' in the evenings and at weekends, while working as a trainee accountant for my day job, developing my portfolio career.

There is now a very fertile base for new business start-ups. It has created a hothouse environment for the gig economy, fuelled by leaps in technology, communications and the disruption of many major industries.

Current UK statistics about businesses

As there are several forms of running a business, from (for example) self-employment, through private limited company and partnership, the statistics are sometimes difficult to pin down. The statistics are collected through different sources, but the numbers below summarise the major issues.

Businesses

At the end of 2018, according to the Department for Business, Energy and Industrial Strategy, there were 5.7 million businesses in the UK, up from 5.5 million the previous year. Of those businesses, 99.3% are classed as small businesses with fewer than 50 employees.

Micro businesses with under ten employees make up 96% of private sector companies.

Small and Medium Enterprises (SMEs)

The biggest industry sector for SMEs (0 to 249 employees) is the service sector. With many types of services being covered, it accounts for 74% of businesses. The construction industry accounts for 18% of businesses.

Self-employment

According to the Office for National Statistics (ONS), the latest figures during writing show that 4.8 million people were self-employed in 2017, a rise of 1.5 million since 2001.

The vital economic importance of SMEs

SMEs are vital to the UK economy. They generate 51% of all UK business turnover and employ 60% of the working UK population (*UK SME Data, Stats & Charts Q3 2019 Merchant Savvy).*

Successful new businesses invigorate the UK economy, and contribute to its dynamism.

Chapter 2 Survival of the fittest – the evolution of success

There is no such thing as good enough. You, your team, and your equipment must be the best. That is how you will win victories.

Gene Kranz – Flight Director of Apollo 11

Survival of the fittest

Business mimics nature by requiring only the 'fittest' to survive. Charles Darwin established the evolutionary principle of 'survival of the fittest' in the 1850s.

This can be described as *Survival of the form that will leave the most copies of itself in successive generations.* In biological terms this is survival of a species in the competitive natural world.

In business, survival means generating enough income and cash to be a 'going concern' and remaining solvent to continue trading in a competitive environment.

Business insolvency

When a business is insolvent, the total debt the business has is more than the value of total assets. Equally, insolvency arises if payment of debts as they become due cannot be made because of poor levels of income or cash flow.

Directors of insolvent companies have major responsibilities and may be held personally liable or be subject to criminal proceedings if they carry on trading fraudulently.

Chilling statistics on business start-up failures

The failure rate statistics on business start-ups do not make for pleasant reading.

Failure rates of new businesses are high:

- 80% of UK companies fail within their first year *(Turnerlittle.com, Companies House data)*
- Only 50% of businesses survive their fourth year, while 44.1% survive for five years or more *(ONS 2011–16)*
- 11.6% of businesses die each trading year *(Merchant Savvy)*
- 381,000 new businesses are being born in the UK every year, while 336,000 cease trading on an annual basis *(ONS 2018)*

It's tough out there!

So, what distinguishes between survival and failure? Clearly there are many factors in play, which we shall examine in more detail throughout this book.

The first thing to note is that there is little margin for error in starting a new business. Risks and pressures are high, and any weaknesses in planning, assumptions or pricing can be catastrophic. Cash resources are usually very limited at start-up and have a finite life. Small, often unforeseen, circumstances distinguish between survival and failure.

The killer blow: businesses fail simply because they run out of money

This is the real reason for virtually all business failures. The management of cash is therefore one of the most important of business activities, especially in the vulnerable early stages. Cash is dealt with in more detail in Chapter 39.

Why do businesses have difficulty in generating cash?

The real question is 'Why do businesses have difficulty in generating enough cash, and then go bust?'

The reasons businesses fail (or do not generate enough cash)

There are many reasons insufficient cash is generated. There are lots of statistics on the numbers of failures, but apparently little UK research is available on the reasons for those failures (besides lack of cash).

Here is a list of some suggestions:

- **Lack of capital and under investment** – a lack of awareness as to how much money is really needed to run the business day-to-day
- **Inadequate management skill** – lack of business acumen of the business owner or management team
- **An inadequate business plan**
- **Marketing mishaps**
- **Leadership failure** – an inability to make the right decisions most of the time
- **No differentiation** – no 'unique value proposition'
- **Ignoring customers' needs** – e.g. not responding to, and learning from, negative customer reviews
- **Inability to learn** from failure
- **Premature scaling** – growing the business too fast
- **Poor location** – especially important in businesses that rely on foot traffic
- **Poor financial and cost management** – not knowing where you stand all the time

- **Draining the business** to support a personal lifestyle
- **The wrong team** or partner
- **Starting at the wrong time in the business cycle** – some start-ups are susceptible to prevailing economic conditions
- **Lack of focus** – trying to be 'all things'
- **Lack of profit** – a profit has to be earned for survival, and to fund growth

This is a huge list, with lots of pitfalls for the unwary.

The list also gives a strong flavour of the many 'life-threatening' issues that must be faced in setting up a new business.

Secret No. 1 Cash is always king – no cash, no business

Next Action: Read Chapter 39

Start by being open-minded

Start with an open mindset. Be willing to learn enough to avoid the many pitfalls outlined above.

The aim of this book is to provide insight into setting up a business, and to mitigate or eliminate as many of these risks as early as possible.

Chapter 3 Competition

Competition is the activity or condition of striving to gain or win something by defeating or establishing superiority over others.

The Race to the Moon – Charles Murray

The Apollo Programme was born out of international competition during the Cold War in the 1950s and 1960s. The spur that drove the USA to the Moon was the concern that the USSR would get there first.

Business competition

Business competition is the battle between businesses to win customers and sales. Competition benefits customers, as businesses are under constant pressure to improve their product or service offering at competitive prices.

Businesses can be competitive in these areas:

- Price
- Customer and user experience
- Cost
- Location
- Brand
- Sales force capability
- Technology
- Reputation

Competitive advantage

Competitive advantage comes about when a business can do something better than its competition. There are many types of competitive advantage, particularly in today's marketplace where mature businesses can easily be wrong-footed by lower cost disruptors using technology.

Competitive disadvantage

Competitive disadvantage comes when a business will lag behind the competition, for example, because of higher costs, wrong location, outdated products etc.

Your business idea

Start with a clear view of what competitive advantage you have. For example, a better or cheaper service, higher quality products, or faster delivery.

Consider your competitive position in a clear-sighted and professional way. Failing to address these issues at the outset will potentially kill your business down the line.

Secret No. 2 Think clearly about your competitive advantage in your business plan

Next Action: Include your competitive advantage in your business plan

Chapter 4 Gaining 'The Knowledge' and understanding how to run a business quickly

The key to good decision-making is not knowledge. It is understanding. We are swimming in the former. We are desperately lacking in the latter.

Malcolm Gladwell – Journalist and Author

Trade and professional qualifications

Many trades and professions have formalised products, services and qualifications. As an example, to become a London Taxi Driver, candidates learn 320 routes and points of interest within a six-mile radius of Charing Cross. They are then tested by examination and a further practical test on suburban routes. This process usually takes between two to four years to complete and involves much riding of London streets, usually on a moped, to learn the routes. This is known as 'The Knowledge'.

A driver passing The Knowledge can set up in business easily, acquire a vehicle, then drive out to ply for hire. The vehicle markets itself, and the driver is in business.

Other trades and professions such as plumbers, hairdressers, accountants and lawyers have entry requirements. We will talk more about barriers to entry in Chapter 17.

How long does it take to become expert in your field?

Malcolm Gladwell, in his best-seller *Outliers*, popularised a rule of thumb that it takes 10,000 hours of practise to master a particular art or major skill. His theory was based on the number of hours violinists took to reach expert proficiency. His idea neatly side-stepped the ability factor involved, but the '10,000 Hours' has become a by-word for the length of time it takes to become expert in a particular field.

Chess Masters – an example of learning a skill

Further work in this area by some psychologists (*Gobet F. & Campitelli, G. 2011 Deliberate Practice: Necessary But Not Sufficient 2011*) with Master Chess Players found there were huge differences in the number of hours of practise taken to reach Master Chess Player status – from 728 hours to 16,120 (the equivalent of around four and a half months to nearly eight years).

Why are Chess Masters relevant?

A possible conclusion to draw would be that some people can become Chess Masters quickly, while others can never achieve it, as it would take too long. In business, there is very little learning time, so the parallel is important. Those who learn and adapt quickly will win, those who take too long to learn will go bust.

Applying your expertise in a new setting

Running a business requires having major expertise or knowledge and converting that knowledge into a marketable commodity, whether it is a service or a physical product. We will call it 'product knowledge' (which covers either physical or service products).

A new business start-up propels that 'product knowledge' into the commercial world, untried and untested. It requires launching, with marketing and promotion from the owner, who may have no previous experience of running a business.

Learning to run a business from scratch in 10,000 hours?

My assertion here is that the learning curve for starting a new business from scratch has the same requirements as becoming qualified in a trade or profession. It will take time to learn the business skills needed, and experience to overcome the challenges.

Time is of the essence

My conclusion is that, although perhaps not directly comparable, the chess analogy indicates there is little time to learn how to run a new business.

With slow learning, and a run of unforeseen problems, the business probably fails. However, the positive alternative is that with good preparation and being aware of the issues to be covered at the outset, the new business gets more than a sporting chance to succeed.

Secret No. 3 After launch, there is little time to get a new business right before it potentially fails

Next Action: Read Chapter 33 and have a clear list of actions that can be achieved before launch

Chapter 5 What do you know about running a business?

Reports that say that something hasn't happened are always interesting to me, because as we know, there are ***known knowns;*** *there are things we know we know.*

We also know there are ***known unknowns;*** *that is to say we know there are some things we do not know.*

But there are also ***unknown unknowns****—the ones we don't know we don't know. And if one looks throughout the history of our country and other free countries, it is the latter category that tend to be the difficult ones.*

Donald Rumsfeld – US Secretary of Defense, February 2002

What we think we know

What do you know about running a business? You may have worked in a business as an employee, and already have a view as to the everyday challenges that face the managing director or the boss.

If you have not run a business before, the direct knowledge you have will be relatively small, (what you 'know') and may have been obtained third hand or by hearsay.

The big trap to avoid is knowing what you 'don't know' and being clear about what you think you 'know'.

This requires being open-minded and willing to learn. It also needs the ability to get the knowledge needed to run the business well enough in time to avoid any major pitfalls.

Thinking about the knowledge needed to run a business, the diagram below gives an insight into the knowledge we have.

Knowledge of running a business

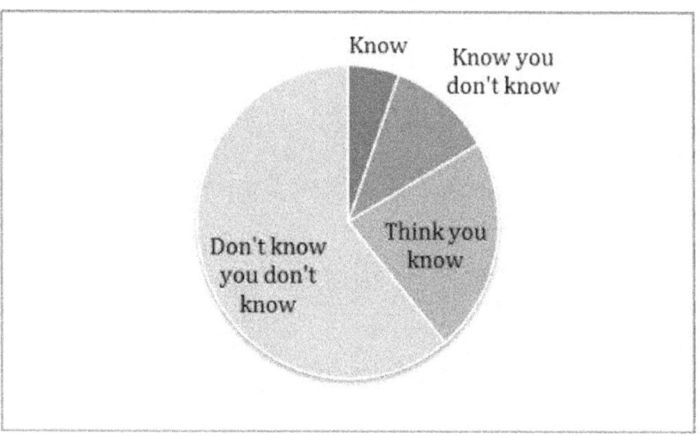

protectedtree.com

This can be further summarised by the 'Circle of Knowledge' diagram below, which simplifies the position with more clarity.

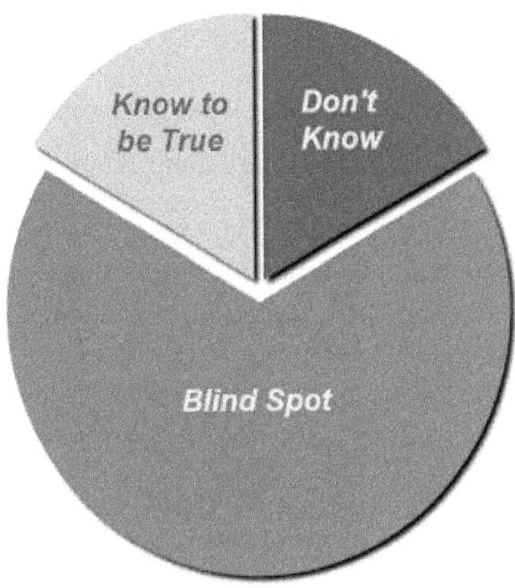

Finney & Associates

There is a huge potential blind spot in knowledge which could lead to business failure if it is not addressed. Clarity, and reducing the size of the blind spot using clear understanding will reduce risk and potentially solve business problems encountered on the way. We will talk more about 'solutions not problems' in Chapter 10.

Secret No. 4 Address your business knowledge – eliminate the blind spot and learn what you don't know

Next Action: Think about the limits of your knowledge, and look to improve in areas that need work

Chapter 6 The stages of starting a new business

I've never been able to contemplate failure. Success is everything.

Raymond Blanc – Chef Patron, Le Manoir aux Quat'Saisons

Even though there could be little time to get things right after a business has launched, there may be the luxury of plenty of time available in the run-up to the launch.

The table below shows my view of the early stages of starting a business.

I have used the Apollo parallel, as there are many similarities in setting up a project from scratch with a clear objective, but not having the immediate expertise or knowledge to deliver it.

The early stages of starting a business

The Early Stages of Starting a Businesss						
	1	2	3	4	5	7
Stage	**Initial Idea**	**Mission**	**Planning**	**Launch**	**Survival**	**Expansion or Exit**
Risk Level	Very Low	Very Low	Very Low	**Very High**	**Very High**	High
Milestones	Concept	Proof of concept	Final Business Plan	Launch	Survival	Preparation for Exit
	Initial ideas	Idea tested	Funding	Monitoring	Monitoring	Monitoring
		Desk research	Logistics	Meet Key Launch deliverables	Change business plan?	Review and replan
		Market testing	Due Diligence			Team Building
		Draft business plan	Final reality checks			

The first three stages are 'very low risk', and risk levels are 'very high' or 'high' from launch onwards.

We will look at timing and preparation in more detail later, but the reality is that more time spent in preparation will reduce risk after launch.

Risks after launch are 'very high', and any mitigation which reduces the risk of becoming one of the 50%+ failures in the first five years, is time very well spent.

Secret No. 5 Do as much preparation, learning and understanding before launch as possible, to reduce risk

Next Action: Build risk reduction into your plan and develop your ideas

Company birth and death rates

Risk for new businesses also varies by sector and region. The ONS has published the birth and death rates for companies across different sectors for 2018 (in thousands):

Company births and deaths 2018 by industry group

Birth and death rates by broad industry group
UK, 2018

Counts given to the nearest thousand

	Active	Births		Deaths	
	Count	Count	Rate (%)	Count	Rate (%)
Production	174	18	10.1	16	9.4
Construction	389	50	12.9	39	10.0
Motor trades	85	9	10.2	7	8.3
Wholesale	116	10	8.8	10	8.5
Retail	255	43	16.9	31	12.1
Transport and storage (inc. postal)	135	24	17.8	22	16.5
Accommodation and food services	184	28	15.5	24	13.3
Information and communication	256	32	12.7	27	10.4
Finance and insurance	46	6	12.4	5	10.7
Property	119	15	12.9	13	11.2
Professional, scientific and technical	542	63	11.7	61	11.3
Business administration and support	278	48	17.2	43	15.4
Education	45	5	10.8	4	9.3
Health	121	10	8.1	16	13.4
Arts, entertainment, recreation and other services	193	19	9.6	16	8.4
Total	2,940	381	12.9	336	11.4

Source: Office for National Statistics – Inter-Departmental Business Register

Failure rates for companies in Transport and Business Administration, for example, are roughly double the failure rates for Production and the Motor Trades.

What is the failure rate for your sector? If it is relatively higher than average, what can you do now to reduce the risk, and what will you do differently?

Location is also a factor

Where your business will be in the UK will also affect risk. The ONS analysis shows that the North West and the West Midlands have higher rates of failure than other geographic areas.

The same approach applies as with industry sector – if you plan to start a business in a more challenging region, ensure that your planning specifically mitigates that challenge.

Company births and deaths 2018 by region

Birth and death rates by region
UK, 2018

Counts given to the nearest thousand

	Active	Births		Deaths	
	Count	Count	Rate (%)	Count	Rate (%)
North East	76	9	12.5	8	11.0
North West	301	43	14.3	41	13.5
Yorkshire and The Humber	198	23	11.8	22	10.9
East Midlands	189	23	12.1	21	10.9
West Midlands	236	31	13.3	31	13.1
East	292	36	12.3	31	10.6
London	613	97	15.9	78	12.7
South East	450	53	11.7	45	10
South West	232	24	10.4	22	9.5
Wales	105	14	13.3	11	10.4
Scotland	186	21	11.1	22	11.8
Northern Ireland	61	6	9.6	5	7.9
Total	2,940	381	12.9	336	11.4

Source: Office for National Statistics – Inter-Departmental Business Register

Secret No. 6 Know your sector and geographical risks, and how they can be addressed

Next Action: Look at the data for your sector and area, and note how those risks can be mitigated

Part 2 – Are you suited to running your own business?

Chapter 7 What is an 'entrepreneur'?

Nobody talks about entrepreneurship as survival, but that's exactly what it is and what nurtures creative thinking. Running that first shop taught me business is not financial science; it's about trading: buying and selling.

Anita Roddick – founder The Body Shop

Origins

'Entrepreneur' is a French word from the early 19th century, originally denoting the director of a musical institution. It has been adopted by English language speakers more recently to mean:

A person who starts a business and is willing to risk loss in order to make money.

Are entrepreneurs born or made?

This debate has been going on for many years, with some notable entrepreneurs dropping out of school or university to build large corporations, such as Richard Branson (Virgin) and Steve Jobs (Apple).

There are, however, many other entrepreneurs who 'transitioned' into entrepreneurship after the age of 30.

In a report *'Nature or Nurture' (2011)* of 685 entrepreneurial leaders, Ernst & Young found:

- Nearly 60% of entrepreneurs described themselves as 'transitioned' from a corporate environment
- 45% of entrepreneurs started their first business after the age of 30

Ernst & Young commented that:

Nurture not nature does appear to be more important in shaping the entrepreneurial mindset.

Anyone can learn to be an entrepreneur

So, the majority of entrepreneurs have transitioned from an existing 'day job'. This shows that anyone can learn how to start and run a business.

Life, however, is not that simple, and there are personality characteristics which will help an aspiring entrepreneur, and other traits that will hold them back or contribute to business failure.

A fantastic entrepreneur in hospitality

Raymond Blanc came as a young man to the UK from France in the 1970s, working as a waiter. He had no formal training as a chef but opened his first restaurant, Les Quat'Saisons in Oxford in 1977.

He mortgaged his house, and borrowed money from 18 further people. With overnight success (Egon Ronay Restaurant of the Year and two Michelin stars), he went on to open a chain of bakeries and patisseries. In 1983, he opened Le Manoir aux Quat'Saisons, the world famous, Michelin two-starred restaurant.

Raymond Blanc helped to change the restaurant culture in the UK and went on to train many other notable chefs and restaurateurs, including Heston Blumenthal and Marco Pierre White.

Secret No. 7 Anyone can learn to be an entrepreneur, and run their own business providing they have the right personality traits

Chapter 8 What are the characteristics of a successful entrepreneur?

Formal education will make you a living; self-education will make you a fortune.

Jim Rohn – Motivational Speaker

Be an all-rounder

What does an entrepreneur need to be like to succeed?

Taking on a wide range of tasks, some outside the comfort zone, is important. Think of it like athletes in track and field events. The sprinters specialise all their training to meet their one goal of a better time, whether it is in the 60, 100 or 200 metres sprint.

The all-rounders come into play in competitions like the Heptathlon, with seven events covering many sporting disciplines. Points are awarded on a set scale, and the Heptathlon events are:

1. Javelin
2. Shot Put
3. 800 Metres
4. Long Jump
5. 200 Metres
6. 100 Metre Hurdles
7. High Jump

Heptathlon athletes have to train across all their disciplines to maximise their advantage. They are excellent performers in most of the seven disciplines but will lack some attributes to perform in all the disciplines to the highest level. It is about doing a good job across the range and maximising the points scored, by training to improve the weaker events, while outperforming in their strong events.

The Heptathlon: Katarina Johnson-Thompson

Katarina Johnson-Thompson (KJ-T), a GB athlete, brilliantly won the Gold Medal in the Heptathlon at the World Championships in Doha in 2019. Her performance by event is shown in the table, with a comparison against the specialist world record for each event.

Katarina Johnson-Thompson Heptathlon World Championship 2019 Performance			
Event	**KJ-T 2019 World Title Performance**	**Specialist World Record***	**KJ-T % Achievement of World Record***
Javelin metres	43.93	72.28	61%
Shot Put metres	13.86	22.63	61%
800 Metres	02:07.27	01:53.28	89%
Long Jump metres	6.77	7.52	90%
200 Metres	23.08	21.34	92%
100 Metre Hurdles	13.09	12.20	93%
High Jump metres	1.95	2.09	93%
Heptathlon Points	6981	7291	96%
		** Correct at time of writing*	

KJ-T's performance in five of the events is world class, achieving 90% of world record achievement across five of the seven sports.

The 2 events in which she performs less successfully, the Javelin and Shot Put, normally require more body mass, and are potentially more challenging, .

As an example, in the Shot Put, the world record holder (at the time of writing), Natalie Lisovskaya weighs 105kg. This gives her a substantial advantage in putting the shot. By comparison K J-T weighs 70 kg.

A different mix: same result?

My theory here is that providing performance in the weaker events exceeds an 'acceptable' or 'viable' level, then a different mix of performance across the seven events can be successful.

It is clear, though, that a poor performance in one event would be catastrophic at a high level of competition.

Secret No. 8 Your business is like competing in the Heptathlon – prepare to succeed at all the events, not just the sprint

Next Action: Establish which areas need work to achieve a good performance

Chapter 9 Personal skill sets and stocktake

If you want to be an entrepreneur, it's not a job, it's a lifestyle. It defines you. Forget about vacations, about going home at 6 pm – last thing at night you'll send emails, first thing in the morning you'll read emails, and you wake up in the middle of the night. But it's hugely rewarding as you're fulfilling something for yourself.

Niklas Zennstrom – founder Skype and Kazaa

What are the key skills needed in running a business?

Business is an all-round competition like the Heptathlon. My view is that, like the Heptathlon, there are Seven Key Skills needed to run a business.

Seven Key Skills – the 'Heptathlon Challenge'

These key skills are:

1. Motivation and mindset
2. Problem-solving skills
3. Ability to learn, understand and improve
4. Management skills
5. Customer-facing skills
6. Commercial skills
7. Administrative skills

This is the 'Heptathlon Challenge' – there is a need to deliver in all skill departments, or, as in the Heptathlon, the competition will be lost to the best business all-rounders over the seven events.

Inevitably, people can rarely deliver all the skills that cover all seven areas on starting a business.

There will always be areas that need to be worked on, like K J-T working on the Shot Put and Javelin but ensuring that the top 'events' do not suffer either. This can be a real juggling act, but overall success depends upon covering all the bases effectively.

Key attributes

So, what are the key attributes for someone starting a business? Here is my view:

- **A Problem-Solver** – 'Solutions not Problems'. We will deal with this important point in Chapter 10
- **Pragmatic not dogmatic** – a pragmatic person is practical and lives in the real world. A dogmatic person follows the rules and articles of faith without challenge
- **Good judgement and decisiveness** – the ability to make the right (and generally difficult) judgement call when there is sometimes no real 'right' answer and little information available. Often, business decisions have to be made under pressure, without 'full' information being available
- **Tenacity** – a level of stubbornness and 'stickability'. This is essential to battle through the tough times
- **Striving to achieve goals**, – the ability to finish work or projects is vital to making a new business work. This includes working the hours needed to make things happen
- **Drive, passion and belief** – the ability to share that passion with others and infect staff and customers with enthusiasm
- **Ability to spot opportunities** – having enough knowledge to identify business opportunities
- **Happy taking risks** – particularly the potential risk of loss of money

- **Control and autonomy** – wanting to take control and be the boss
- **Creativity** – bringing fresh approaches and new ideas
- **'The Knowings'** – learning, researching and understanding what is relevant and useful to the business
- **Flexibility** in approach – a 'what works' or 'what do I need to do differently' mindset
- **Commitment** – not giving up
- **A 'maverick' streak** – to go against convention
- **Disciplined** –keeping on track
- **Open-minded** – being open to new ideas and no 'not invented here'
- **A 'Self-starter'** – being able to work without instruction
- **Competitive** – wanting to win
- **Strong people skills** – empathetic and good with people

I have mapped the key attributes below in a matrix which shows my view of the relationships between the Seven Key (Heptathlon) Skills and the list of key attributes.

The table may look complicated but shows that the cluster of skills and attributes towards the top left-hand side of the table look to be most important.

The importance and power of 'Knowledge and Problem-Solving skills' also becomes apparent (see below). The table also shows that self-motivation and problem-solving are some of the most important attributes.

Many skills, such as commercial or administrative skills, may be learned, but problem-solving, and motivation are generally innate human characteristics. Problem-solvers could naturally self-select themselves to set up in business.

Key attributes mapped vs. key skills

	Motivation and Mindset	Problem-solving skills	Ability to learn, understand and improve	Management skills	Customer facing skills	Commercial skills	Administrative skills	Total
Knowledge			1	1	1	1	1	5
Problem solver	1	1	1	1				4
Pragmatic not Dogmatic	1	1	1	1				4
Good judgement and Decisiveness	1	1	1	1				4
Ability to spot opportunities	1	1	1					3
Tenacity	1							1
Striving to achieve goals	1							1
Drive, passion and belief	1							1
Happy taking risks	1							1
Control and Autonomy	1							1
Creativity		1						1
Flexibility	1							1
Commitment	1							1
A 'Maverick' streak	1							1
Disciplined				1				1
Open Minded		1						1
A 'Self Starter'	1							1
Competitive	1							1
Strong People Skills					1			1
Count	14	6	5	5	2	1	1	34

Skills stocktake

Going back to the Heptathlon example, understand your personal strengths and weaknesses in the seven events necessary to perform well in business. As a first step, run a personal assessment against the Seven Key Skills, marking each skill out of 10 in the table below.

There are no right and wrong scores – the purpose of this approach is to establish whether the key building blocks for the business are in mind, and for the assessment to be part of the journey towards business success.

Key Skills - Personal Assessment	
	Score Out of 10
Motivation and mindset	
Problem-solving skills	
Ability to learn, understand and improve	
Management skills	
Customer facing skills	
Commercial skills	
Administrative skills	
Total	

Clearly, few people will score highly in all these skills, but some attributes may compensate , such as having a strong personality which may offset other areas.

The important thing here is to know the skills that need work, and to improve them or acquire them. This could include learning more about how to overcome particular problems, or by, say, employing team members who have different skills. It could require buying in skills from outside the business, such as administrative or commercial expertise.

Secret No. 9 Know your own skills, and find inventive ways of plugging skill gaps in your potential business

Next Action: Establish key skills that need further work

Chapter 10 'Propose Solutions Not Problems'

You cannot operate in this room [Houston Mission Control] unless you believe that you are Superman, and whatever happens, you're capable of solving the problem.

Gene Kranz – Flight Director Apollo Programme

Business is about solving problems

A successful business is about solving problems quickly and effectively. You could sit in a room and discuss the problems of setting up a business for many months or years and find many reasons for not acting, and never ever set the business up.

My business background and career were strongly based on 'Propose Solutions Not Problems'. As a discipline it provided a robust structure to help generate lots of alternative solutions to the business issues and problems of the day.

What is the definition of a business?

There are many definitions of what a business is, and usually they are simple:

Business is the activity of making one's living or making money by producing or buying and selling products such as goods and services.

Wikipedia

The statement is true, but in real life it is a little bit more complicated. For a business to survive and thrive in a competitive environment, it has to inherently offer solutions to attract customers at a price that it can make money and generate cashflow.

Business is about delivering solutions

Business is really all about solving problems and delivering solutions that the customer is prepared to pay for. Think of a typical example we may use every week, without being aware of the complexity.

A typical Tesco superstore will stock around 40,000 product lines, of which 25,000 are food and beverages. *(USDA Supermarket Chain Profiles 2016).*

Think about the thoroughness and the problem-solving that has gone into the logistics alone, to ensure that the vegetables, meat and fish are fresh, and that the bread is not stale. Tesco offers grocery solutions at a store near you that we all take for granted.

'Main purpose of job: to propose solutions'

During my early career, I was very fortunate to work for a very well-managed company. It was my first board appointment, as Finance Director, and the job description was a revelation.

The first item in the job description was:

MAIN PURPOSE OF JOB

(Describe the job's purpose in one sentence if possible.)

To propose solutions.

Proposing solutions

In that job, developing solutions took priority over everything else. In the early days, I had to learn a new and radical approach. The boss was not interested in hearing about the problems. Anybody could regurgitate what was wrong and why it could not be fixed.

It takes talent and discipline to be positive, but the environment was steadfast. Those team members that could only talk about the problems quickly fell by the wayside, while those who produced solutions thrived.

The atmosphere in the business was very positive, with the team solving massive problems and consistently beating targets.

Being positive and solutions-driven as a team does work. It helped me have the right approach when I came to set up my first business.

Secret No. 10 Be solutions-driven to achieve success

Next Action: Adopt a problem-solving approach: i.e. 'what are the solutions to this particular problem?'

Chapter 11 The downsides – why running a business is challenging

Timing, perseverance, and ten years of trying will eventually make you look like an overnight success.

Biz Stone – Co-founder of Twitter

Is the grass greener?

It is relatively easy for an employee to look out at the job market from the security of their employment and to assume that the 'grass is greener' running one's own business. From an employee's perspective, a business may be perceived as being in the 'green grass', but a business must always deal with world realities. A business will always look out for the next order and the next customer. An employee can be insulated from the real business world to a greater or lesser extent.

Insecurity

Another argument put forward by employees is that they believe themselves to be in secure employment, but in reality, they only normally have three to six months' job security.

Are jobs more secure for employees than running a business? Is it better to have multiple possible options for future work (with good marketing), rather than one chance of compensation for job loss, which might happen?

However, running a business can be a highly insecure option, particularly for those new businesses not well equipped to survive.

Will a new business make it?

The first few months, as we have shown in earlier chapters, are high risk for new businesses, with a high rate of failure.

An employee may have experience and skills that will be of great value to a new business, but will they be able to generate new business regularly, or will they become just another transient businessperson on their way back to becoming an employee again?

Working outside the comfort zone

When an owner of a new business has tried working outside the employment comfort zone, many questions can only really be answered by embarking on this journey, such as:

- Is running a new business right for me?
- Which niche, specialism, product or service will deliver the best results?
- What can I do best?
- Can I manage the stress?
- Can I manage the financial risk?
- Can I compete in the market?
- Will the market buy what I can deliver?
- What is the market for my products or services?
- Is the market large and buoyant enough to generate the cash my business (and family) needs?

Being uncompromisingly single-minded but broadminded at the same time

If a new businessperson asks the questions about going into business, and thinks *'this is for me, I can do this'*, they will already tend to be self-selecting; they will be purposeful, single-minded and confident in their own ability, possessing very specific attributes that will ensure later success. They will also be broadminded about the commercial world and their place in it.

So, what are the main differences between being an employee and running a business?

Running a business requires a broad spectrum of skills that may often lie outside an individual's experience, comfort zone and expertise (think about competing in the Heptathlon). An employee hoping to create a new business needs to understand that running a business does not suit all comers as the pressures can be substantial.

The table shows my view of the major differences in generic characteristics between employees and businesspeople, which mostly centre on the need to be proactive, solutions-driven and to move quickly and decisively:

Businesspeople and employee generic characteristics

Employee generic characteristics	Businesspeople generic characteristics
Experienced	Experienced
Knowledgeable	Knowledgeable
Excellent work ethic	Self-starter, results orientated
A 'company' person	Independent minded
	High emotional intelligence
	Influencer

Excellent attendance and punctuality	Punctual and reliable
	Good negotiator
	Solutions-driven
	Thinks outside the box
Delivers what is required	Delivers results quickly
	Risk taker
	High enthusiasm and energy levels
Fits into the organisation	Leader, but also team player
	Ability to multitask
	Challenge the status quo
	Apolitical

This summary emphasises the substantial differences in very simple terms. Businesspeople must do more than employees. Vitally, they need to move more quickly than employees to succeed.

Running a business is so much more than a job

So, running a business is very different from being an employee. It normally has both much higher levels of work activity and a greater variety of complex issues to handle. There is also a substantial entrepreneurial element required, which involves some challenging multitasking and critical timing.

The illustration below shows a simplistic, but accurate view of what employees do. Businesspeople must do an awful lot more than employees – doing the job, making the product or delivering the service is only one relatively small part of a much more complex overall picture.

Managing these tasks and their timing is vital. A successful businessperson will develop an innate 'gut' sense of timing and decisiveness.

As a simple example, if a business does not market and sell at the right time, they may well not generate enough revenue and the appropriate cash flow. This will be a recurring theme throughout the book.

Running a business is tough

Running a business is tough. There is pressure to perform across all the seven major Heptathlon events, and to deliver for customers while making sure there is enough cash in the bank to pay the mortgage or the rent at the end of the month.

Business owners do more – a lot more!

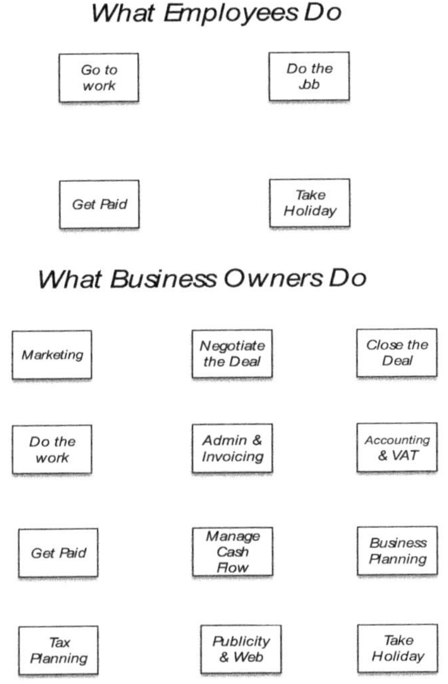

Business owners do much more

Business owners have much more to do than employees on a day-to-day basis. As well as running the front office dealing with customers and the work in hand (see Chapter 36), they have their own back office to run (see Chapter 38).

Being able to multitask and being both highly aware and sensitive to key timing points' for the back office functions are key ingredients for success. Concentrating on customer delivery (the front office) without thinking about paying the VAT or marketing for new work can clearly be catastrophic.

Because of this complexity, and constant juggling, some people that are happy to multitask are well suited to running a business, while others will find it challenging.

Make an honest self-assessment of how closely as a person you match the characteristics needed to run a successful business. One key to success is understanding the linked elements of the business and doing the right things at the right time. The wrong things at the wrong time simply do not work.

Secret No. 11 Sensitivity to key timing points and the ability to respond are major ingredients of business success

Next Action: Establish what your key timing points are likely to be

So, what can go wrong if some of these key timing points are missed, and why is it important?

Forced to take a long unpaid summer holiday

What happens if a customer contract finishes in June, for example, in consultancy, and the business has failed to do the appropriate marketing? Marketing during the holiday period in July and August will normally be an uphill struggle, and the business may be without work until the market picks up again in the Autumn – probably mid-September or later. This could cause a long, unpaid summer holiday, which diminishes any surplus cash reserves.

Hitting the ground running

The 'getting your feet under the table' time that an employee can use to settle into a new job does not exist in business. The new business has the clear objective of 'hitting the ground running'. The business job is about making an impact from day one, demonstrating a clear, planned trajectory that will create a positive cash flow.

Being able to negotiate

A business owner must negotiate and price contracts with customers if in a face-to-face business. Some people may find this level of personal negotiation potentially embarrassing or difficult (see Chapter 37).

Negotiating prices is not straightforward. To state to a customer in a face-to-face meeting that the price of the product or service is £xxx, requires nerve, planning, knowledge and strength of purpose, and the correct sales pitch. Dealing with this important element in a detached, professional and informed way will clearly bring benefits.

What are the results of failure?

There is no room for failure, as a failing business will not generate enough cashflow, and will become another statistic.

This compares unfavourably with the situation of a failed employee, who may remain employed within their employer's 'comfort blanket' for some time, depending on a wide range of factors.

The lack of room for failure in the business world adds substantially to the daily pressures, particularly in a new business with an ambitious business plan.

Self -Reliance

Being in business is also potentially a solitary experience with little or no infrastructure, support, and often no status. Self-reliance and the ability to bounce back from adversity are fundamental attributes of a businessperson.

Ultimately, an entrepreneur can only fall back on themselves, and their own infrastructure, network or partner to deal with the challenges met.

Secret No. 12 Self-reliance and the ability to bounce back from adversity are fundamental to business success

Recognition of reality is not failure

There will be many people considering a business career who find that living and working with so many unknowns will be impossible or too stressful for them. Dealing with the 'unknown unknowns' can be the ultimate challenge for any business. The safe prospect of being employed and being paid regularly may seem very appealing.

People considering running a new business may think that the comfort of a regular payment is how to go, and they either fall out of the new business market or never enter it. This should not be seen as failure, but a recognition that everyone has their own style of working and needs the right structure within which to optimise their own talents and skill set.

Chapter 12 The upside – why running a business is fantastic

I thoroughly enjoy running my own business.

Anonymous

We have looked at some challenges of running a business and seen why being an entrepreneur is not an easy option. In compensation, there are substantial upsides, both personal and financial, for a successful entrepreneur.

A 'made to measure' career

A successful entrepreneur could, over time, generate a lifestyle difficult to match in terms of personal freedom and choice. This flexibility comes from being independent.

Independence, freedom of choice and control

One of the most important benefits of an entrepreneurial career is that it provides independence, control, and perhaps more freedom of choice than a conventional career. For me that freedom was mainly around following my own 'star' and working in sectors I found fascinating and having the chance to work with great people. I also changed industry sectors relatively easily and relished both the challenge and opportunity that came from that change.

My enjoyment also came from having no ties or obligations to a specific corporate way of life, or the political baggage that goes with it. I could follow my own work interests and be free of office politics, which was a major benefit.

Lifestyle, income potential and flexibility in how it's taken

An entrepreneur can decide when and where to work, and also when to take holidays.

As an employee, the opportunities for gaining any flexibility in terms of payment of salary are very limited. Certain amounts must be paid monthly in tax and national insurance, and pension contributions are generally fixed. The effective opportunities for salary sacrifice and fringe benefits are reducing over time and are likely to have been maximised.

Optimising net income

Depending on the legal business vehicle used, the flexibility of having a gross income from a business, and, for example, having to draw only what is needed for living expenses is powerful. Cash can be built up in the business as protection for possible slow periods, or for other expenditure. Time can be taken to plan and optimise net income at key timing points, coinciding with expenditure, business year ends and tax years. Running a business well can help achieve personal financial goals.

This flexibility (which clearly depends on each entrepreneurs' circumstances and the business vehicles used) cannot be stressed enough. The opportunities to maximise, say, pension contributions, cash retention, payouts for capital projects or other spending are generally broad and beneficial. There is a price for this flexibility, which is the lack of security, and the requirement to make a success of the business.

An end to boredom, and regular challenge renewal

A business career is not boring, but exactly the opposite. It can be frenetic, and is often very challenging, requiring intellectual, mental and physical stamina. New challenges generally arise as the business progresses, and there is little time for boredom. This level of constant challenge is very invigorating.

Learning opportunities

There will be many opportunities to learn about the seven disciplines of running a business (the Heptathlon), which is a major element for personal development.

Non-financial rewards

As well as financial rewards, non-financial rewards come from working with great customers and suppliers. I worked with some exceptional customers, but also delivered very interesting projects which had a significant impact. Being in business is also very good for network development, particularly with professional advisers such as lawyers and accountancy firms, and external bodies.

Building teams

Often, I would work alone in my consultancy business with the client. But in some roles, as well as working with some excellent client teams, I also had the mandate, freedom and opportunity to build my own team to deal with some specific projects. This was generally where my solo resources needed leveraging to gain more traction and impact.

These projects covered different businesses in different sectors and were generally troubleshooting roles where time was of the essence to solve a major problem. I adopted the principle of finding the best team member for each role required, and 'setting them loose' so we could then solve the clients' problems together.

This way of working leverages up a business's scope and influence with results being achieved more quickly by gaining traction across a broad range of areas and issues for the customer.

The overall business experience

An entrepreneurial career is a great learning experience that keeps on giving. It is about learning what works and knowing how to implement it, having developed a better and deeper understanding of complex issues and how to solve them.

Secret No. 13 Achieve a great lifestyle running a successful business

Part 3 – Starting a business – what is the mission?

Chapter 13 What are the 'Six Questions' that need to be asked?

I keep six honest serving-men
(They taught me all I knew);
Their names are What and Why and When
And How and Where and Who.

Rudyard Kipling – Just So Stories 1902

The Five 'Ws' + one 'H'

You may think that if you are starting a business, you know already exactly what you will do, and you need not bother with a mission statement. You are going to be a builder, a plumber, a management consultant or sell video games, and that is it. That is fine, but it only describes what the business does, no more.

It does not describe how the business will compete, which, as we have seen before, is one of the most important elements of success.

There are 'Six Questions' that can help enormously in this process, the five 'Ws' and one 'H', immortalised by Rudyard Kipling in his *Just So Stories.*

The 'Six Questions' will add important detail

These six words help add detail to the initial business idea.

Let's imagine a fictional new businessperson, Plumber Sam is starting a business as a jobbing plumber, and has no business ideas, other than wanting to be independent.

Plumber Sam's initial ideas

Who?	Just me
What?	Plumbing
When?	Start next month
Where?	Within a 10-mile radius of home
Why?	To be independent
How?	Not sure

Has Sam answered the important questions? Maybe there should be more thought about the detail? There are many traps for the unwary – we know this from business failure rates.

Who?

Sam's 'Just Me' may not cover what the business needs. Will a plumber's mate be needed to help with heavy work? Will a network of other tradespeople be needed that can help with projects, such as carpentry or tiling? Does Sam have a partner who can help with the administrative tasks?

What will the business do?

What product or services will your business provide?

Sam's answer is 'plumbing'. This is a very general answer, but probably means 'general domestic plumbing installations, repairs and maintenance'.

Sam's training covers this (and as you can see, we have already tightened Sam's business focus).

When?

Timing is everything. We have seen earlier that time spent on planning before the launch of a business is low risk. There is every reason to delay a business start if corrections can be made to the plan to reduce risk.

Where?

Sam wants to work locally (within a 10-mile radius), and clearly thinks that the local market is big enough or uncompetitive enough to support the business. Is this right?

Is there a shortage of plumbers in the area – do they all make a good living?

Why?

What are Sam's motivations? Would Sam be better off being an employee? Has Sam thought about the reasons for going into business?

How?

We assume that Sam wants to do general domestic plumbing and is qualified both formally and with experience to do so. Sam seems to take a 'potluck approach' about the kind of work that will be found.

The 'How' and the 'Why' are fundamental

'How' your business does what it aims to do is fundamental to your future business success and should include your personal core values and approach.

Are you planning to do business in a particular, unique or special way? Why are you doing that?

Another plumber starts a business

Having looked at Sam the Plumber, let's take another fictional example of Plumber Chris, who starts a business, but takes a different approach.

	Plumber Sam	**Plumber Chris**
Purpose	To be a jobbing plumber	To help customers improve their energy efficiency
How?	Provide plumbing services as required	By installing the best systems to help reduce customers' energy consumption
Why?	For Sam to make a living	To help the planet by installing the best energy efficient systems
Vision Statement	To make a good living	In five years' time to be the first port of call for householders in the county to improve their domestic energy efficiency
Mission Statement	Reduce my borrowings	Help save the world

Which of these start-ups will have a greater chance of success?

Secret No. 14 Answer The Six Questions carefully

Chapter 14 The mission statement

I believe that this nation should commit itself to achieving the goal, before this decade is out, of landing a man on the Moon and returning him safely to Earth.

John F. Kennedy – President of the USA 25th May 1961

Great clarity in a few words

This one mission statement by President Kennedy put in train a process that saw 12 people land on the Moon over an eight-year period. It took 400,000 people, working on the project and cost $28bn in the 1960s, which adjusted for inflation today would be around $288bn (£222bn).

President Kennedy had a clear vision of what he required. The Cold War with Russia was at its height, and he urgently needed to recoup the competitive position in space that the USSR had gained with Sputnik, and the first manned orbit of the Earth by Yuri Gagarin in 1961.

I'm not going to the Moon – why do I need a mission statement?

The mission statement helps entrepreneurs think about what they are trying to do. It also will help clarify your objectives. Believe it or not, physically writing the mission statement down, and showing it to others (not potential competitors) has great benefit.

Many of the failures of new businesses can be blamed on not having a clear enough view of what the business did or was trying to do.

'I have a dream'

You may well have had a dream for starting your new business. Transferring that dream into reality takes a lot of thought and hard work, and it is worth spending time to translate your dream or aspiration into a practical, workable format.

As we have seen, doing more planning work before setting up the business has a big potential to be beneficial. I would urge you to refine your dream again and again. This can be done with good research, dealt with in Chapter 16.

'It does what it says on the tin'

Look for a short statement with great clarity. It will take time to develop and evolve, as writing something short and punchy is much more of a challenge than writing pages of material. If you look at the examples here, they are short, powerful, and clearly say what each business aims to do:

Mission statement examples

Google: 'To organise the world's information and make it universally accessible and useful.'

Starbucks: 'Establish Starbucks as the premier purveyor of the finest coffee in the world while maintaining our uncompromising principles while we grow.'

Twitter: 'To give people the power to share and make the world more open and connected.'

Secret No. 15 Refine your business dream again and again to be a short, punchy and powerful statement

Next Action: Write your dream down in one sentence

Chapter 15 Which business model will you use – 'traditional' or 'disrupt'?

As a result of the digital age and the decline of first-class mail, there is no question that the US Postal Service must change and develop a new business model.

Bernie Sanders – Senator US Senate

What business model will you use?

The business model is an important concept to understand and is what drives how all businesses work.

A business model is defined as:

A plan for making a profit. It identifies the products or services the business will sell, the target market it has identified and the expenses it anticipates. (Investopedia)

A business model is much more than just a plan to make a profit. I think it is the accepted way that businesses are structured and how they operate in their markets.

If you think back, many businesses have traditionally operated with a supply chain with different levels between supplier and customer. Over centuries, say in manufactured goods, this has been the traditional chain that new businesses have entered at one of five levels:

1. Raw material supplier
2. Manufacturer
3. Wholesaler
4. Retailer
5. Customer

The 'traditional' plumbing business model

Going back to the example of Plumber Sam – if Sam was to be asked about the business model, the reply would be 'I'm a traditional Plumber'. This generally means setting up as self-employed, opening an account with a plumbers' merchant, buying supplies at a trade discount, and then selling them on at retail or discounted prices, including adding labour charges to customers.

This would be a traditional business model approach, one that has existed for many years.

We would, however, hope that Sam would now use technology for the front office parts of the business for marketing e.g. Checkatrade or MyBuilder, and mobile systems for invoicing, banking and accounting for the back office.

'Disruptive' models

With new technologies, there are now many businesses using 'disruptive' business models with great success.

Disruptive business models create disorder in the market by giving customers products and services that they demand but have been ignored by the leading providers and manufacturers of that industry. Disruptors provide product and service solutions which the current (usually mature industries) have failed to deliver.

Major examples are:

Amazon – the retail sector

Uber – Taxi business

Netflix – TV and entertainment

Airbnb – Accommodation

Monzo – Banking

Dyson – Vacuum cleaners

Tesla – Electric cars

These businesses have succeeded in their disruption and have quickly become giant companies with explosive growth.

Their business issues are generally not about survival, but how quickly they can grow or 'scale' their operations to keep up with demand and go on to dominate their markets.

'Hybrid' business models

Hybrid business models use a half-way house between the traditional model and the disruptive model. Perhaps a good example is Costco, who's idea was to eliminate the wholesaler in its supply chain:

1. Manufacturer
2. Retailer – Costco
3. Customer

Costco started in the USA in 1976. It opened its first UK warehouse in 1993, and now has 29 warehouses in the UK. Worldwide it has 785 warehouses and 99.9m members, with annual sales of $152.7bn. Costco stocks 4,000 items compared to the average of 30,000 found in most large supermarkets. By concentrating on a few products, it can offer best value to its members.

The Costco mission statement

Costco's mission is:

to continually provide our members with quality goods and services at the lowest possible prices.

In order to achieve our mission, we will conduct our business with the following Code of Ethics in mind:

- *Obey the law.*

- *Take care of our members.*
- *Take care of our employees.*
- *Respect our suppliers.*

If we do these four things throughout our organisation, then we will realise our ultimate goal, which is to reward our shareholders.

Think how much business Costco have won from traditional retail and wholesale suppliers by having a great business model. They have also successfully scaled up their operation on a global basis.

Traditional businesses are now always under tremendous pressure

Disruption is taking place all the time in most sectors. It is a major driver for new business start-ups, as the rewards and opportunities can be immense. We have seen the rapid success of Amazon and Uber, with traditional businesses coming under more competitive pressure from new disruptors. Barriers continue to be broken down, with many opportunities arising.

Disruption is an opportunity and a threat – beware using an obsolete business model

New start-ups taking a traditional approach should think carefully how competitors could disrupt them in the future. There is no point in setting up a new business, with a model that may become obsolete in a few months or years.

Sam the Plumber might want to think about how business plans might benefit from technology or how the plans might be put at risk.

Secret No. 16 Carefully choose a business model that can be competitive in an era of enormous change and 'disruption'

Next Action: Think about how your business idea can be strong, and disruptive if possible

Chapter 16 Research, research and research

Time spent on reconnaissance is seldom wasted.

Arthur Wellesley (Duke of Wellington) – Victor of the Battle of Waterloo 1815

The 'Knowings'

How can you learn what you need to know about running a business?

We know that running a business is complicated, with the seven 'Heptathlon' events to cover, and also the 'Six Questions' that need to be answered. Fortunately, many answers to our questions are readily available on the internet.

There was once a time, in the last century, when if you needed information, you had to visit a library and look up reference books usually long out of date. Now we can discover what we need to know quickly, after learning a few basic skills.

I call finding this knowledge 'The Knowings'. Finding and learning 'The Knowings' is fundamental to the new business journey and potential future success. Not understanding 'The Knowings' is a recipe for potential disaster.

The internet is a fantastic free resource

Today, you can discover anything you need to know from the internet, barring commercial secrets (and you might find some of those). The internet and social media are tremendous resources.

Search engines

Search engines are an outstanding free resource. They require learning how to ask the right questions and knowing where to look on the internet for the answers to particular questions.

This book is not the place to provide a lesson on how to use search engines effectively – there are many other places to discover that. The important point, however, is being prepared to ask a search engine many questions on the same theme. This will enable you to drill down into the information you need to find.

Use the 'Six Questions' from Chapter 13 as a starting point to build up a picture and a personal library of good information. You can keep screenshots in different photo files to keep a record of your findings for the future, referenced by subject, if you need to.

Secret No.17 Refine your search engine questions to sift and find the nuggets of knowledge that you really need amongst the huge volume of information

Next Action: Try different approaches to your searches

Specialist sources

There are other specialist sources of business information such as COBRA Cobweb Information (Complete Business Reference Adviser). COBRA researches a number of small business sectors and produces over 100 guides, ranging from barber shops to restaurants. The research covers start-up; legislation and regulation, performance indicators; and accountancy.

Companies House

One of my favourite resources online is Companies House. It is very useful for discovering information about the competition, suppliers and customers, if they trade through a limited company.

You might think that you do not need to know about Companies House for your new business. It is a huge source of free, valuable information about competitors and suppliers. It will be very useful to learn more detail, especially if you are planning to have a limited company to trade through, or your competitors or suppliers run limited companies.

When do companies have to submit accounts?

Limited companies are normally required to submit accounts to Companies House within nine months of their year-end for private companies, and six months for public companies.

What are the different sizes of companies?

Companies are split into different size categories for Companies House:

- Micro-entities – turnover less than £632k, balance sheet total less than £316k, and ten employees or fewer
- Small Company – turnover less than £10.2m, balance sheet total less than £5.1m and 50 employees or fewer

- Medium Sized Company – turnover less than £36m, balance sheet total less than £18m, and 250 employees or fewer

Why is this important?

All companies have to submit a balance sheet and a profit and loss account, but in general smaller companies only need to produce 'abridged accounts'.

This means that the accounts usually show restricted information, so you cannot necessarily find the turnover (sales) figures for a company but you can look at the balance sheet.

How much cash does my competitor have?

The balance sheet can provide very interesting and revealing information:

- How much cash is there?
- Are there any assets, such as property?

This information, although usually a little old, is extremely useful background information about competitors, customers or suppliers.

An example

Here is a real example of Companies House information for one small company, which has been anonymised:

Abbreviated Balance sheet
As at 31st October 2015

	Notes	2015 £	2014 £
Fixed assets			
Tangible assets:	3	**18,554**	782
Total fixed assets:		**18,554**	782
Current assets			
Stocks:		**65,748**	38,427
Debtors:		**45,581**	7,452
Cash at bank and in hand:		**45,008**	-
Total current assets:		**156,337**	45,879
Creditors			
Creditors: amounts falling due within one year	4	**158,173**	55,837
Net current assets (liabilities):		**(1,836)**	(9,958)
Total assets less current liabilities:		**16,718**	(9,176)
Total net assets (liabilities):		**16,718**	(9,176)

It looks like 2015 was a good year, with £45,000 cash in the bank, and net assets of £16,700.

So, what happens later?

Balance Sheet
as at 31 October 2018

	Notes		2018 £		2017 £
Fixed assets					
Tangible assets	3		11,008		11,012
Current assets					
Stocks		-		31,242	
Debtors	4	10,197		27,330	
Cash at bank and in hand		-		2,404	
		10,197		60,976	
Creditors: amounts falling due within one year	5	(91,269)		(68,705)	
Net current liabilities			(81,072)		(7,729)
Net (liabilities)/assets			(70,064)		3,283
Capital and reserves					
Called up share capital			100		100
Profit and loss account			(70,164)		3,183
Shareholder's funds			(70,064)		3,283

There has been a roller-coaster ride, and in 2018 the business owes £91,000 (including a £53,000 overdraft and £32,0000 in tax) and has net liabilities of £81,000.

Would you lend money to this business if it were your customer?

Would you lend money to this company as a customer, or would you be happy to rely on them as a supplier?

The example shows this information is very dynamic, and changes constantly. Having done your Companies House checks, think seriously about buying information from a credit rating agency about your customers and suppliers.

Secret No. 18 Use Companies House to check up on your competition, customers and suppliers for free

Next Action: Check out your biggest competitor on Companies House

Who owns the company?

Other major questions that can be answered from the Companies House website are:

- Who owns the majority of shares in the business?
- What other companies are they involved in?
- Are there any borrowings?
- Are the borrowings guaranteed by charges on property or other assets?

This information is free and available quickly at the click of a mouse. It is well worth investigating.

Social Media

Social media is great for learning about the market and competition. LinkedIn, Facebook and Twitter are valuable sources of information. Again, screen shot and file useful information for later reference, if needed.

Research continues over the life of the business

Research is a continuing discipline that carries on over the life of the business. You can never know enough about your market competitors and industry. Being on top of what is developing provides a superb competitive edge.

Secret No. 19 Become a great researcher, and an expert on your business

Next Action: Follow your market and future developments to help business success

Chapter 17 Barriers to entry

The brick walls are there for a reason. The brick walls are not there to keep us out. The brick walls are there to give us a chance to show how badly we want something. Because the brick walls are there to stop the people who don't want it badly enough. They're there to stop the other people.

Randy Pausch – Professor, Carnegie Mellon University, USA

What are barriers to entry?

Barriers to entry are obstacles that prevent new participants or competitors from gaining easy entry to an industry or area of business. These barriers benefit existing businesses already operating in that market.

If your proposed business has substantial barriers to overcome, be strong and persistent, as overcoming the barriers is worth the fight.

There are four primary barriers to entry:

- **Resource ownership** – do I own the machinery needed to produce a product, or the mine to produce the mineral?
- **Patents and copyrights** – do I have to develop my own unique new product to avoid infringing patents?
- **Government restrictions** – how can I get on the list of approved government suppliers?
- **Start-up cost** – how can I raise the money to build a new factory from scratch to compete?

There are other barriers, which include:

- **Technology** – special technology needed to make a particular product

- **Economies of scale** – mass production costs are usually tiny compared with higher small batch costs
- **Access to supplier and distribution channels** – does my business qualify for a trade account and the highest level of discount with a supplier?
- **Professional accreditation** – have I the right qualifications to ply my trade?
- **Competitive response** – will competitors play tricks to eliminate new competitors like me?
- **Mindset** – how can I ever compete with them?

Procurement policies and rules: beware large organisations and government

Larger organisations, both public and private, generally have inflexible procurement rules. These can work against new businesses that need to act quickly. A lot of time and money can be used up seeking potentially good deals with larger organisations that take a long time to reach fruition, or that may never appear.

In large organisations there is often a big contrast here between the urgency of the need of the organisation, and the organisation's ability to swiftly procure a solution.

Smaller organisations often have more autonomy to make fast decisions and make an ideal target for new small businesses starting up as clients.

Fewer barriers for disruptive businesses?

New disruptive businesses may have fewer problems overcoming barriers to entry. For non-disruptors, it is worth accepting that it will be a fight to overcome the barriers, but that the fight can be worthwhile, as many potential competitors may well fall by the wayside trying.

'Jumping through the hoops'

Jumping through the hoops is a necessary part of setting up a new business. Only those with enough commitment to not give up manage it, which is why it is usually a mindset issue.

Barriers to entry generally help reduce the number of competitors in a particular sector, so once the barriers have been overcome, many businesses go on to thrive. All the effort, pain, time and trouble becomes worthwhile.

Secret No. 20 'Jumping through the hoops' is a necessary part of starting a business. It shows commitment and staying power

Next Action: Establish a plan on how to overcome your barriers one by one

Chapter 18 Working capital

Annual income twenty pounds, annual expenditure nineteen nineteen and six, result happiness. Annual income twenty pounds, annual expenditure twenty pounds ought and six, result misery.

Charles Dickens – David Copperfield

What is 'working capital'?

I want to stay away from complex accounting principles and formulae but some understanding of working capital and how it works is fundamental to business survival.

We have seen in Chapter 2 that businesses fail from lack of cash. This generally means cash in the bank or other items which convert easily to cash, such as stock or money owed to the business (receivables). These are current assets.

Working capital represents the difference between a business' current assets and current liabilities (the money due to be paid out for suppliers, tax etc.).

When starting a business, it is essential to have the level of working capital required to operate solvently. This means having enough margin of liquid cash to survive any delays in payment from customers or to accelerate payments to suppliers (to e.g. maintain supply).

The challenge with working capital is that some parts of it are flexible to manage, while others are not.

The simple example below shows a working capital surplus of £100, so if the business was wound up today, all other things being equal, the shareholders would retain £100 for their efforts.

Working capital example

Current assets	£	How flexible?
Cash	100	Liquid
Receivables (Debtors)	100	Subject to payment terms and customers
Stock	100	The right stock is convertible to cash
Total	300	
Current Liabilities		
Payables (Creditors)	100	Subject to payment terms and suppliers
PAYE	50	Has to be paid on time
VAT	50	Has to be paid on time
Total	200	
Working capital	+100	Surplus

The main point in this example is that the only really flexible thing in the balance sheet is cash. The remaining items have to be managed carefully to become usable assets:

- receivables need chasing to be paid
- stock needs to be sold, and cash released

The liabilities also have to be managed so they do not become expensive or dangerous, for example:

- Expensive: HMRC issue automatic fines if PAYE or VAT is not paid on time
- Dangerous: creditors refuse to supply or take legal action if not paid

The first cash flow model is vital

Getting working capital right at the start of a business is challenging, and one reason why time should be spent on planning and cashflow.

We will talk more about cash management in Chapter 39.

Chapter 19 Ethics

It takes 20 years to build a reputation and five minutes to ruin it. If you think about that, you'll do things differently.

Warren Buffet – CEO Berkshire Hathaway

What are ethics?

The dictionary definition is that ethics are *'moral principles that govern a person's behaviour or the conducting of an activity.'*

Business ethics

There are three main elements to business ethics:

- **Human values** such as care of employees, fair advertising, value for money and fair treatment of shareholders and business partners
- **Business activity** such as fair competition, and non-discrimination
- **Global activity** such as product testing and branding

Ignore ethics at your peril?

There were times in the 1980s City of London when 'ethics were a county near London'. More recently, with social media and opportunities for mass communication and boycotts, the protection of corporate reputations is vitally important.

In 1994, John Elkington, an American economist and entrepreneur, proposed his concept of a 'Triple Bottom Line' in business. He maintained that any business should be based on three fundamentals:

1. Sustainable development
2. Social and environmental issues
3. Financial probity

Businesspeople and companies sometimes ignore the first two fundamentals at their peril.

VW 'Dieselgate'

A good example is the Volkswagen (VW) 'Dieselgate' scandal. VW deliberately deployed software that rigged pollution emissions for 11 million cars worldwide. VW were given a criminal fine of $2.8bn in April 2017 in the USA, with directors facing criminal charges.

VW have suffered immeasurable reputational impact to what had been a very strong brand, built up across the world after World War II.

Corporate social responsibility

Employers looking to align their values to a more ethical standpoint, as well as keeping up to date with ethical values can be accredited with Corporate Social Responsibility (CSR) through formal schemes that demonstrate the four pillars of CSR:

- Environmental
- Community
- Workplace
- Philanthropic

Why are ethics important for a new business?

When a new business starts, it will be with the entrepreneur's values attached to it from the outset. As the new business matures, it will need to develop a more formal approach to business ethics and CSR.

Ethics in the 21st Century

Businesses in the 21st century will increasingly need a strong ethical base. As climate change and environmental issues rise up the agenda, new businesses will need to make very clear exactly where they stand.

Secret No. 21 Develop a positive approach to business ethics, as they become more important over time
Next Action: State the ethical position of your business in one paragraph

Chapter 20 Help and assistance – mentoring and non-executive directors

Be strong enough to stand alone, smart enough to know when you need help, and brave enough to ask for it.

Ziad K. Abdelnour – Corporate Financier

Everybody needs help

Starting a new business is tough. We have seen in earlier chapters there is much to learn, and that it is challenging to get a clear view of all the issues to understand.

This chapter is about who to talk to for help and advice. Clearly, if you are still employed, you will need to consider who you can share your aspirations with carefully. However, the value of sharing your ideas with others who have experience of business start-ups is immense.

Types of contacts for help

1. Local business support groups
2. Your network
3. Professional bodies and institutions
4. Business incubators and accelerators
5. Mentors
6. Non-executive directors

Local business support groups

There is a great network of local business support groups, which are easy to find, and easy to contact for help. As an example, my local group, Buckinghamshire Business First (BBF), is dynamic and very helpful.

BBF has over 11,500 small, medium and large business members, runs four business hubs, and offers over 80 business events every year. They are a tremendous resource for help and business feedback. They also offer help with mentoring, business planning and advice.

Your network

There will be people in your network who will be able to help or put you in touch with others if they cannot. Your network may have some members already involved in the business you are looking to start, so there is potentially a lot of added value.

Professional bodies and institutions

These are a natural port of call if you are looking to practice a profession or formal trade as they will have specific codes of practice that will need to be adopted.

Business incubators and accelerators

According to *smallbusiness.co.uk*, there are around 300 business incubators in the UK supporting about 12,000 businesses. Incubators generally specialise in start-up companies, and can often be linked to the educational sector, particularly universities. There are major benefits for new businesses, including mentoring, grants and office space.

Business accelerators take a more proactive approach, and usually have deeper involvement in the new business. They often take an equity stake of around five to ten percent in the business and aim to grow each business rapidly. They operate typically in the technology sector usually for a period of up to a year. According to *entrepreneurhandbook.co.uk*, there are over 180 accelerators in the UK.

Do it now – make contact and go to the meetings

Go to the meetings and be prepared to talk about your ideas, and to make changes as you go along. Do not be concerned about your lack of experience, as nearly everybody in the room will be in a similar situation to yourself.

Pitch your idea

At meetings, you will get to pitch your idea to people for a reaction. This is great practice for when you have to pitch for real, and also you could get valuable feedback, particularly from those local entrepreneurial organisations that help business start-ups.

Mentoring

What is mentoring?

A mentor encourages, motivates and helps a mentee towards achieving their goals. Usually, mentors meet their clients once a month for perhaps an hour.

The Prince's Trust

I started my mentoring career with The Prince's Trust (TPT). TPT do a fantastic job in supporting the start of new businesses by young people. They get help with small loans but require a clear business plan and a mentor to be appointed. The mentor usually meets the client once a month, over two years.

Does mentoring work?

In 2016, TPT published some research in partnership with NatWest Bank, called *'Trust in Business'*.

TPT had supported over 80,000 young people to set up in business. They surveyed 550 entrepreneurs two and three years after start-up.

The results are very clear, with 76% still running their business after two years, and 73% after three years.

This compares with the 80% of new companies failing in their first year we saw in Chapter 2.

Mentoring clearly substantially helps new start-ups.

Use a mentor if you get the chance

In my experience, most start-ups unfortunately do not use mentors regularly. There is possibly some resistance on grounds of cost, and a big 'unknown' factor in choosing a mentor.

For a new entrepreneur, it is often difficult to overcome the hurdle of cost, as well as the difficulty they may feel in sharing private details of a new business with a stranger. The actual cost, however, is very low – the equivalent of a half-day fee per month, but the potential benefits are substantial – possibly survival over failure.

Where mentoring is offered as a package, for example with a loan, both the mentor and the entrepreneur quickly adapt to a very productive relationship, helping the new business substantially.

Secret No. 22 A mentor will help – your business is much more likely to survive, and to succeed

Next Action: Find a mentor through your contacts or local business support organisations

Non-executive directors

A non-executive director (non-exec) does not get involved in the day-to-day management of a company, but is involved in strategy, planning and helping the company achieve its goals.

A non-exec is similar to a mentor, but on a much more formal basis. In a large start-up, non-execs can bring great weight to strengthen an inexperienced board of directors, particularly in negotiation, raising finance or strengthening public perception.

The essential requirement is obviously having a sufficiently interesting, strong and valid proposition to attract a non-exec to the start-up board.

Part 4 – Starting a business – planning the mission

Chapter 21 A final mission plan, budget and cash flow

There is no such thing as good enough. You, your team, and your equipment must be the best. That is how you will win victories.

Gene Kranz – Apollo Programme Chief Flight Director, Houston

Why should I produce a plan, budget and cash flow?

- Until a plan is written down you only have aspirations
- Before you risk your own cash you need to see how much money the business will make in theory

A good business plan is one that is well thought-through, covers all the essentials and provides a firm foundation for success. For one-person businesses, it is important to know exactly where the money will come from to pay the mortgage (or the rent) in six months' time after start-up.

A start-up without a plan is just a dream

As we have seen earlier, many dreams lead to great businesses being started. It takes courage to write down the ideas, and to formalise what is just a concept or dream.

The act of writing things down is very powerful, even if it is difficult to put your plan on paper. You skip this bit at your peril, and risk becoming another failure statistic.

The plan gives a firm foundation for success

The plan should show the major challenges for the business, and how they will be dealt with.

We all know that real life will be different, and that the plan will change over time as the business evolves. Producing a plan makes the writer think about both the upsides and downsides of the business, improving both 'The Knowings', judgement and decision-making.

The discipline of writing a plan, and having it read by associates or colleagues might confirm or deny that it is a good business idea.

Formalising plans

A fully rounded business idea should be formed, and quite a lot of research will have taken place. People will have been consulted, questions asked, and a 'feel' gained for whether the business will work.

There will be a belief that the business idea is possible, and now is the time to formalise the idea for the first time.

How to make a start – a simple tool: 'COM'

As we have seen earlier (the 'Six Questions' in Chapter 13), knowing what questions to answer helps to focus the mind in the complex business planning situation.

To cut through the complexity, I have used a very simple tool for my entire career for solving business issues called 'COM'.

What is 'COM'?

COM is a simple framework in which you put your problem to solve (i.e. the business plan). This format is very flexible and can be easily expanded:

C =Current Situation:

- Market
- Competition
- Pricing
- Personal finance
- Etc.

O=Objectives:

- Set up a new business
- Turnover of £x, in year one
- Etc.

M=Method

- Outline the 'How'

Start with a 'COM' on two pages of A4

I always aimed to get the initial thinking on any 'COM' into one or two pages of A4. This is a great start, which can then be enlarged to populate a detailed business plan template.

How much detail should I go into?

The level of detail required will depend on the complexity of the business idea, the number of partners involved and whether any external funding is required.

Other simple tools to use

The Business Model Canvas Template (Miro) is a free tool, available on the internet, that is a good way to link different strands of a business plan together.

Raising money from the 'Dragons'?

The business plan that Plumber Chris' would have produced will be very different to a plan taken to raise finance from the 'Dragons' on BBC TV.

Both, however, benefit enormously from having done the work. If Plumber Chris has problems with finance, bank funding is likely to be found more easily by using the business plan. The applicants to the Dragons will know their business better, having written a detailed plan, and should be able to answer those difficult questions that the Dragons throw at candidates, more easily.

Levels of planning detail

The complexity of the new business proposition can be categorised into four main types, which range from:

1. **Straightforward:** one-person business, self-financed
2. **Intermediate Single:** one-person business raising finance
3. **Intermediate Multi**: start-up with partners/shareholders, self-financed
4. **Complex**: start-up with partners/shareholders raising external finance or invitation for corporate partners

Which type of business plan do you need?

	Type	Plan	Budget	Cash Flow	Suggested Page Length
1	**Straightforward**	Simple	Simple	Simple	5
2	**Intermediate Single**	Detailed	Detailed	Detailed	15
3	**Intermediate Multi**	Detailed	Detailed	Detailed	15
4	**Complex**	Complex	Complex	Sophisticated	30+

The Straightforward Plan would include two to three pages of rationale (possibly in COM form) a one-page budget and a simple cash flow.

At the other end of the scale, the Complex Plan could be perhaps over thirty pages with appendices covering five-year forecasts for the profit and loss account, balance sheet and cash flow.

Business plan templates

The aim of this book is not to tell you how to write a business plan. It is to point the reader in the right direction, having seen which type of planning is required.

There are many templates available online. The reader can decide which type of plan they wish to produce, and then populate a suitable template, ensuring that all the key areas are covered in enough detail for their type of business.

Plans take time to evolve but give great credibility

In mentoring new start-ups, I have been involved in complex business plans. One start-up had, for example, 17 versions produced of the Business Plan (over 50 pages with appendices) during a 12-month pre-launch period.

This was a lot of work for the founders and was a real journey. The benefit was that, at the end of the process, the founders not only had a confident view of business prospects, they also could effortlessly answer any question about their plan. When facing 'Dragons' or the bank manager, or making a pitch, this is a substantial win.

Secret No. 23 A written business plan, appropriate for the size and complexity of your start-up will provide external credibility and increase your knowledge of the business

Next Action: Try drafting a business plan suitable for your type of start-up and get feedback

Chapter 22 Unique selling points (USPs)

That's one small step for man, one giant leap for mankind.

Neil Armstrong – First man on the Moon

Being first on the Moon, Neil Armstrong was famously understated about winning the race to the Moon for the USA. USPs are explained below, but they are about winning in a competitive, commercial situation.

USP – A unique selling point (or proposition)

A USP is a unique selling proposition that differentiates a product or service from its competitors. It makes your business different from all the others in the market and helps your business proposition stand out. It helps make the business competitive and will attract customers.

Some examples of USPs are:

Fever Tree: 'Premium tonic water.'

Domino's Pizza: 'You get fresh, hot pizza delivered to your door in 30 minutes or less, or it's free.'

FedEx: 'When it absolutely, positively has to be there overnight.'

USP Factors

USPs can be a combination of different factors, or a single factor. Some of the factors are:

Personality – such as Jamie Oliver, Richard Branson

Process and content – e.g. handmade organic local cheese

Special services – free delivery, customer loyalty scheme, 14-day guarantee

Niche target audience – e.g. Weight Watchers, Saga

Location – specialist local knowledge

Product – premium or luxury product like Fever Tree tonic water

Ethics – environment, charity

Distribution – different distribution from competing products

Trust – use qualifications or endorsements to differentiate – e.g. Checkatrade, MyBuilder websites

Pricing – luxury items sell for higher prices

What are you doing differently from your competitors?

In Chapter 13, we compared Plumber Sam and Plumber Chris starting on their business journey. What USPs should they both think about?

We have seen that Plumber Sam's initial business idea was:

General domestic plumbing, repairs and maintenance.

Plumber Chris had developed his business ideas further:

To help customers improve their energy efficiency.

In the table below, Sam's and Chris's aspirations are compared by the USP categories shown above. This helps bring out the reality of what the terminology means in practice.

Who has the most powerful USP differentiation?

Plumber Sam and Plumber Chris – USP development

	Plumber Sam	**Plumber Chris**
Personality		
Process & content		Energy saving advice
Special services		Show payback on energy saving
Niche target audience		'Green' customers
Location	10-mile radius	Within the county
Product	Standard products	Energy saving products
Ethics		Environmental
Distribution		
Trust	MyBuilder, Checkatrade	Personal recommendation
Pricing	Market	Premium?

Clearly Chris can show a stronger, more compelling selling proposition than Sam, as it is more specialised. Chris is also likely to be more proactive in selling projects, rather than reacting to breakdowns.

Chris could have potential to grow the business over time by, say, opening accounts with specialist energy efficiency suppliers, and also potentially offering finance through third parties based on energy savings and so on.

Sam, however, is likely to remain a reactive jobbing plumber, which is fine if that is what is required. Sam will need to hope there will never be too many plumbers operating in the local area, and that the plumbing business is immune from the disruption of chains (such as Pimlico Plumbers).

Chapter 23 SWOT analysis

To recognise that the greatest error is not to have tried and failed, but that in trying, we did not give it our best effort.

Gene Kranz, – NASA Flight Director, Apollo 11

What is SWOT analysis?

SWOT is a classic business tool that has been used for a long time. SWOT analyses a business under four headings:

1. **S**trengths
2. **W**eaknesses
3. **O**pportunities
4. **T**hreats

Strengths and weaknesses are mainly internal

Think about the strengths and weaknesses being mainly internal factors about you and your proposed organisation. For example, what skills will you or your new team bring as entrepreneurs? What are your weaknesses, and what areas should you learn about?

External – mainly opportunities and threats

Opportunities and threats are mostly external factors, such as the market, technical developments, the economy and the competitive position of your new business.

Be honest – who are you trying to kid?

Without real honesty, these exercises can end up a sham. To a degree, we all like to kid ourselves about things, but to be valuable, 'kidology' should play no part in SWOT. Kidding yourself or your team is a recipe for losing money (lots of it). Look to have brainstorming sessions with your team or your partners to establish clearly where you stand.

What is brainstorming?

Brainstorming is defined as:

An activity or business method in which a group of people meet to suggest a lot of new ideas for possible development.

I used brainstorming as a very valuable technique, both to provide new solutions, ideas and approaches, but also to help bind people together into a problem-solving team.

Brainstorming rules

There are many ideas about what brainstorming rules to have. What worked for me was simple:

- A clear period of time – at least two hours
- Clear, simple agenda
- No interruptions from outside
- No judgements or negativity – any idea is valid
- Have a facilitator if possible
- Everybody encouraged to contribute
- Use a white board, smart board or pad – be visual
- Notes, conclusions and next actions circulated quickly

A continuous process of brainstorming

An established business from my experience would normally review the SWOT analysis once a year, and brainstorm through it in, say, an afternoon. It would be updated regularly. Brainstorming should become a continuing process and part of the planning cycle, which is adjusted year-by-year as the business changes. Research the latest ideas on how brainstorming can help your business.

What are strengths?

Strengths are things you do well, skills you bring, or things that give competitive advantage:

- What will you do differently from your competition?
- How do you differentiate your business from the competition?
- What brings your business clear advantage over the competition?
- Do you have particular personal skills, like marketing and closing a deal?
- Does your team have good internet or IT skills that can give competitive advantage?

And so on. Your USPs are also strengths.

What are weaknesses?

Every business has weaknesses. Knowing about them and writing them down, though, is a different matter. We have seen how limited our knowledge can be **(What we know we don't know)**.

Weaknesses also cover areas that a new entrepreneur may know nothing about **(What we don't know we don't know)**, such as:

- Ignoring finance: cash flow, PAYE, VAT and taxes
- Lack of sales ability
- Administration and company reporting deadlines
- Legislation affecting the business

We have seen the Seven Key Skill Areas ('Heptathlon') that need to be covered to run a business well, and it is important to cover known weaknesses, while thinking deeply about other potentially unknown weaknesses. These are important areas for further work, that if overlooked could mean the business becoming another bad statistic.

What are opportunities?

What opportunities can you spot in your market? Do you know of events or developments that you can use to your advantage? What changes are there going to be in your market, affected by demographics (e.g. the growing aged population), social change, technology or social media?

What are threats?

Threats are external factors that negatively affect your business, from government legislation, technology, competition and the Coronavirus.

Secret No. 24 In the SWOT analysis, weaknesses and threats need to be covered comprehensively to avoid failure

Next Action: Take time to consider your SWOT, and be brutally honest about Weaknesses and Threats

Chapter 24 Internet and social media

We don't have a choice on whether we DO social media, the question is how well we DO it.

Erik Qualman – US Author

This is not a 'How To Guide' on social media

This book is not about showing entrepreneurs how to 'do' the internet or social media better – there are much better sources of information available elsewhere. The aim here is to cover the essentials, and to avoid some of the major traps.

What internet and social media profile does your business need?

Different businesses have different requirements, but new businesses will need to have an online presence of some sort.

As an example, Plumber Sam will register on local tradespeople websites, and possibly be registered with Checkatrade or MyBuilder. Sam will be available by phone and email. But is Sam ever likely to set up a website?

Plumber Chris, however, is looking further ahead, and may justify the expense of setting up a website, or decide that a DIY website is the answer.

How important will your website be?

Some new businesses will require very sophisticated websites, while others may have no real need for a website. Clearly if the website is mission critical, then either the expertise or the money to develop the internet site must be found.

If the needs are relatively modest, it is possible to take a DIY approach. But beware of the fact that a DIY website may not look or function as well as one built professionally, and the users (customers) may be able to tell the difference.

More sophistication and other ideas

It is possible to run multiple, customisable websites, based on different market segments. These can be split by, say, gender or age at relatively low cost. Much more information is available on the internet or can be found through local business organisations. For example, Nigel Temple (nigeltemple.com), a digital marketing specialist produces a free marketing eBook *300 Ways to Promote Your Enterprise.*

Maintain your website

Businesses often forget to update or maintain their website regularly. There is little worse in business than presenting an out-of-date proposition to their audiences.

Allow enough budget for the website the business needs

How much does a website cost? On a DIY basis, costs can be relatively low, but an 'all-singing, all-dancing' website could cost many thousands or tens of thousands of pounds to set up.

Think about branding and the user experience (UX)

UX is defined as *'the overall experience of a person using a product such as a website or computer application, especially in terms of how easy or pleasing it is to use'. (English Oxford Living Dictionaries)*

UX is important for your website, in ease of use and appearance, but it is also more subtle than that. If your website sells your services or products, users will need to be encouraged and moved in the right direction, to close a transaction.

Your brand will also need to be well presented and demonstrated, both visually and in words. Using graphics and a logo are important and may require external input.

The words (copy) used on websites usually differs in length and style from normal written communications, because of internet page sizes, fonts and the need to keep the viewers' attention. The idea is to persuade users to click through to the next level. Writing those pages and putting them in the right order to communicate the required messages is a specialist skill.

There is more on branding in Chapter 26.

Social media

You may be already on Twitter and/or Facebook, and may have a following. LinkedIn can be used for generating contacts, normally for business-to-business marketing, such as selling professional services.

Secret No. 25 Engaging with the internet and social media is a great tool for building a successful business

Next Action: Think about what digital presence is appropriate for your type of business, timescale, and how much it costs

Chapter 25 Location and co-operative working spaces

The best location we get is right next to a McDonald's. We can compete with them because we do it better.

S Truett Cathy – Billionaire Founder of Chick-fil-A, USA

Location, location, location

For some businesses, location is everything. There may be benefits from good access to customers, suppliers or a local, talented workforce, or good transport links.

The choice of location in one of these hotspots will benefit the business but may also require paying a premium for that location. Think, for example about banks in the City of London, or luxury goods retailers in airport duty free outlets, and the premium rents payable for those locations.

For some other businesses, location can be less important, and the decision could be about the location with the lowest cost, which often comes back to running the start-up from home.

I ran my businesses from home but was fortunate to live within an hour's commute of London, a huge market, which had many benefits.

What affects location?

Some factors that affect location of a business are:

- **Accessibility** – roads, rail and motorways, and parking. Can customers get to you easily, and vice-versa? Are deliveries easy and quick to make?
- **Competition** – locations near competitors can be a benefit – see the quote at the beginning of the

chapter. Fast food outlets are gathered together, so people have more choice, and more customers are attracted. Not everybody may want to eat curry but may like Chinese food or fish and chips instead. Shoe shops experience similar benefits

- **Costs: rent and rates** – premium rents are payable for the best spots in both office and retail
- **Workforce** – do you have access to a workforce with the right skills, if you need it
- **Potential for growth and scalability** – can your location support the growth of your business for the foreseeable future?

Do I need my own premises?

My guess would be that a lot of start-ups could effectively be run from the kitchen table, and so do not need premises. There will be some, however, that need manufacturing or warehouse space from the outset.

Keep the overheads low

Avoiding the need to make a commitment on premises is key, as the cost increases business risk substantially. Think about how that long-term commitment can be avoided, perhaps through sub-contracting manufacture. This is where a solutions-based approach can be the difference between success and failure (think about brainstorming the best options).

Fever Tree plc – a great example

As a long-term policy, keeping overheads low can work well (see Chapter 40). A good example of this approach is Fever Tree plc, the tonic water maker.

Fever Tree, which started business in 2003, turned over £237m in 2018, but has only 135 employees (*Fever Tree plc Annual Report 2018*).

Fever Tree disrupted the traditional soft drinks market with a very successful business model that makes them essentially an ingredients and marketing company. Manufacture and distribution are all outsourced, so they have no manufacturing plant and distribution of their own.

Think for a moment how difficult it would have been to set up a bottling plant, warehouse and distribution network, as well as sourcing all new drink formulations and ingredients.

See Chapter 50 for an update on how well Fever Tree was prepared for the Coronavirus pandemic.

Working from home

Working from home is a good solution, as it is low cost and low risk (but do not forget to get insurance, and any other approvals you may need).

Try and separate a space you can use all the time, with proper lighting, heating and ventilation and a comfortable chair, and a good internet connection.

The downsides of working from home can be 'cabin fever', and lack of human contact. Family circumstances can also affect work, and there generally need to be very clear rules and some formality about the hours of work and interruptions. Customer meetings can be arranged at their premises or neutral locations.

Co-operative or shared working spaces

These spaces, such as hubs and shared working spaces are a great 'half-way-house' between having an office and working at home. They are often subsidised by local authorities and can be free. Their benefit is being able to network with like-minded people and it helps to get out of the house. They usually have a hot-desking arrangement with Wi-Fi, with meeting rooms generally available.

The synergy gained from meeting other people starting up businesses is a great benefit, both for knowledge and morale.

Secret No. 26 The best startup businesses minimise their commitment to premises, while maintaining a good location

Next Action: Think how your business can provide a great product or service without committing to premises

Chapter 26 Intellectual property

You know, sometimes I don't understand what's wrong with us. This is just about the most creative and imaginative country on earth – and yet sometimes we just don't seem to have the gumption to exploit our intellectual property. We split the atom, and now we have to get French or Korean scientists to help us build nuclear power stations. We perfected the finest cars on earth – and now Rolls-Royce is in the hands of the Germans. Whatever we invent, from the jet engine to the internet, we find that someone else carts it off and makes a killing from it elsewhere.

Boris Johnson – Journalist (2010)

What is Intellectual Property?

Intellectual Property (IP) refers to creative work which can be treated as an intangible business asset, similar to physical property. IP rights cover four main areas;

- Copyright
- Trademarks
- Design right
- Patents

How do you own IP?

Below are extracts from the gov.uk website, which is very helpful. You own IP if you:

- Created it (and it meets the requirements for copyright, a patent or a design)
- Bought IP rights from the creator or a previous owner
- Have a brand that could be a trademark, for example, a well-known product name

On ownership, IP can:

- Have more than one owner
- Belong to people or businesses
- Be sold or transferred

If you are self-employed, you usually own the IP even if your work was commissioned by someone else, unless your contract with them gives them the rights.

You usually will not own the IP for something you created as part of your work while you were employed by someone else, as employment contracts often give all IP rights to the employer.

Copyright

You automatically get copyright protection when you create:

- Original literary, dramatic, musical and artistic work, including illustration and photography
- Original non-literary written work, such as software, internet content and databases
- Sound and music recordings
- Film and television recordings
- Broadcasts
- The layout of published editions of written, dramatic and musical works

You can mark your work with the copyright symbol (©), your name and the year of creation. Whether you mark the work does not affect the level of protection you have. So, for example this book is a copyright work, and is protected.

Trademarks and logos

Trademarks are different, because they have to be registered to protect the logo, trademark and the brand. If you register a trademark, you will be able to take legal action against anyone who uses your brand without your permission, including counterfeiters, and put the ® symbol next to your brand – to show that it is yours and warn others against using it. You can also object to new trademarks that are similar to yours.

Classes of trademarks

There are 34 classes of goods trademarks, and 10 classes of services. Some classes are complex – for example:

Class 8 'Hand tools and implements, hand-operated; cutlery, side arms, except firearms; razors.'

Registering a trademark costs money, usually about £200 for each one, plus £50 for each class. A multi-class registration could cost, say, £500. Remember that logos and wording are usually separate marks. Also remember that existing trademark holders can object to your proposed registration, if it has close resemblance to theirs.

The great thing about trademarks is that, once registered, they are an 'intangible asset', and can become very valuable, as well as providing protection for your business.

Design right

'Design right' automatically protects your design for ten years after it was first sold, or 15 years after it was created – whichever is earliest. You can use it to stop someone copying your design.

Design right only applies to the shape and layout (how different parts of a design are arranged together) of objects, and you can also register your design for better protection if it meets the eligibility criteria. You must register a design to protect 2-dimensional designs such as graphics, textiles and wallpaper. Designs can be registered online from £50 for one, with discounts for volume.

Design right has to be proved, usually by keeping certified signed and dated copies with a lawyer.

Patents

A patent application will show ideas behind a product, including how it works, what it does and why. A granted patent gives its owner the right to prevent anyone else producing, importing or selling, within the geographical area to which the patent applies.

Patents are a complex and expensive area that requires special expertise. Much planning will be required to both set up the patents, and then exploit them.

A personal note on patents

I had personal experience of a venture capital-backed start-up that held a patent, that was thought to be high value by the management team and its venture capitalist backers. It turned out to be valueless, and unenforceable, for a variety of reasons which were not at all clear at the outset.

Patents require very clear thinking, top-level advice, and lots of money.

IP Conclusion

If you have IP, protect what you can at reasonable cost as part of your business plan – it may have great value later on.

Secret No. 27 If you have IP, formalise as much of your IP as you can to create an 'intangible asset' of value later on

Next Action: List out your potential IP by category and take immediate steps to protect it

Chapter 27 Teams and partners

It isn't equipment that wins the battles; it is the quality and the determination of the people fighting for a cause in which they believe.

Gene Kranz, Failure is not an Option – *Apollo Programme*

Teams are mission critical

Great teams can do great things for a business. In contrast, individuals not working together in a business can do severe damage to any business.

I'm working on my own – why should I worry about teams?

If you are thinking about running a solo business, the importance of having a strong backup team is vital to business success. You will be in the front line running the business, but in reality, a solo business is seldom run in total isolation.

A solo business

As a solo businessperson, you will need to talk about, and discuss the business with, others at some point. This interaction will give very important perspective about the many decisions you as a solo businessperson have to make.

The 'others' may be your domestic partner (if you have one), friends, parents, a business confidante or mentor, your accountant, banker or your lawyer, or a local business adviser.

Choose your initial advisers well

You can't choose your parents, and you have chosen your partner and friends. It is important to choose other sources of advice well, such as accountants, bankers and lawyers. These advisers should know your plans and be happy to support you in achieving them. Look for empathy and support from them to help you achieve your ambitions and try to get the best value you can from these initial advisers.

If you approach your potential advisers with your well thought-through business plan, they will take you seriously from the outset.

It may cost money to have good advisers, but if you succeed in your business, it is a win-win for both their business and for yours.

Domestic partners

The importance of your domestic partner, if you have one, cannot be emphasised enough. They should be fully 'on board' with your plans and ambitions, as they may become involved in the business. They may find themselves fielding phone calls and rearranging holiday dates. If they decide to become further involved, they might eventually run the back office administrative function for the business.

Starting with a small team

If you are starting a business with a small team, the position is a lot more complicated, and there are several initial challenges to consider:

1. What are the likely shareholding percentages among the team? (see Chapter 29)

2. How much money will each shareholder put in (and do they have the cash)?
3. Who will lead the team?
4. Will all the team be directors?
5. Will all the team be employees?
6. What skills and expertise does the team have?
7. What skills and expertise are lacking?
8. What culture will the business adopt?
9. Who will define team member roles?

These challenges should be addressed in the business plan, which should include the team's CVs and demonstrate how gaps in expertise or skill are being solved. Presenting a strong, multidisciplinary team, particularly to investors or banks, is fundamental.

Building teams

Some of the most exciting and fun times I have had in business have been when building my own teams from scratch and working to help complete projects for a client.

I had three occasions where my client allowed enough budget for me to recruit a team to deliver a project too big for me to handle on my own. Instinctively, I always recruited the highest possible calibre people to work for me, as it had always worked well for me in my employed career. The same principle applied to my own business.

Sometimes, a line manager may appoint a subordinate with less ability, so that the subordinate does not present a current or future threat to the manager. This approach made no sense to me. It made even less sense on a project assignment. It is essential to have the best people to get the best results, which are then a success for all concerned.

I would always start by recruiting through the agencies I knew could do the best search job, and who were on the same wavelength as me (and my support team).

Do not worry if your team members are cleverer than you – their ability can really pay dividends and help accelerate a business to great success.

The quality of the people I found on those three occasions was outstanding. It was a pleasure to share my aims and objectives for the project with them, and then to set them to work to help solve the problems.

Secret No. 28 All businesses need a great team to be successful, even solo startups

Next Action: Think carefully about what your team and advisers bring to the table, and their future potential

Part 5 – Starting a business – on the launchpad

Chapter 28 Legal, tax, and commercial aspects

Warning klaxon!

This chapter is only an outline of what is a very complex area of law and is not to be relied on for detailed technicalities. Always seek advice if you need it.

The structure of the business

A new business needs to be set up properly to meet all legal and tax requirements, and to avoid some traps, such as personal liability and tax issues. This needs proper professional advice, as the downside of getting it wrong can be very expensive.

The main practical structural options currently available are:

Self-employment

A person is self-employed if they run their business for themselves and take responsibility for its success or failure. Self-employed people are not paid through the Pay-as-you-earn tax system (PAYE), and they do not have the employment rights and responsibilities of employees. They pay tax in arrears, and allowable expenses are generally slightly more beneficial than for a limited company.

On the face of it, being self-employed is appealing from a tax viewpoint. The big issue, however, is personal liability. All self-employed people suffer the risk that a customer may sue them personally. All their personal assets, including their own house and property are at risk, owing to their personal unlimited liability to the business.

Depending on the business that the new start-up deals with, and the potential value of errors of negligence that could be made, self-employment could be a 'non-starter'.

Limited company

A new solo business will often set up as a limited company, with the owner usually being both a shareholder and director. The company will invoice the customer for services which generates income. The business then has different options for using that income. These may include taking allowable expenses, paying a salary subject to PAYE, taking taxable benefits in kind, and paying dividends based on the profits of the company.

Specialist options

There are also other, more specialist options available, including umbrella company, unlimited partnership, limited liability partnership, company limited by guarantee and community interest company. All options will require advice.

Limited liability is good

A limited company does what it says – it limits liability. This normally protects personal assets such as houses and pension schemes from attack by a third party.

Any third party suing a limited company, such as for negligence, would normally need to look to a professional indemnity or other insurance for compensation. The insurance company usually has a much greater asset and cash base than a personal limited company.

The downside of running a limited company is that you will need an accountant to help with the bookkeeping and filing of annual accounts at Companies House. Also, as we have seen, your competitors see your filings at Companies House in due course.

VAT and taxation

At the time of writing, the UK VAT threshold was £85,000, with VAT payable if taxable turnover goes over that level.

Remaining below that level for many businesses is important for competitiveness. In hairdressing, for example, going through the VAT threshold would mean a sudden 20% increase in pricing, which may cause a loss of business.

HMRC scrutiny

It is both wise and prudent to expect and plan for scrutiny by HMRC, despite any other factors.

Be prepared to have full details available to defend yourself properly. Good, and detailed, accounting pays off.

I had two HMRC investigations, which were 7 years apart, covering 14 years of my limited company operation. Nothing resulted from these examinations, but I did incur additional professional costs, and lost time going to meetings with HMRC. Insurance is available to cover this eventuality.

Professional indemnity and other insurances

Professional indemnity insurance (PI), also known as PI insurance or indemnity insurance, can help protect a professional (such as a consultant or an accountant) if claims are brought against them by a customer due to a problem with work the professional has done for them. PI will offer cover for compensation that the business may be forced to pay to correct a mistake or cover any legal costs due to negligence, such as giving incorrect advice or making a mistake in their work.

A business may need PI if it:

- Regularly gives advice to clients
- Handles data belonging to a client or business
- Is responsible for a client's IP
- Provides a professional service and could be challenged on its work

Other insurances

A business owner may feel confident in the quality of their work, but any small business is vulnerable to a claim of negligence when professional advice, services or product delivery fails to meet a customer's expectations and cause financial loss.

Businesses can often work on very challenging projects with large sums of money riding on the outcome, so if your customers are relatively large businesses, and if things go wrong, they may have the capacity and the deep pockets to pursue for damages, even if it is rarely done in practice.

Some of these insurances can be purchased at very low cost and provide substantial cover and peace of mind. Consider them if they are relevant to your business:

- **Public liability** – protects against compensation claims and legal costs if injury, death or damage are caused to a third party
- **Employers' liability** – a legal requirement if you have employees, which covers the cost of compensation for employee injury or work-related illness
- **Tools and business equipment** – loss, damage or theft of tools and equipment
- **Contract works** – covers losses due to theft or vandalism on construction sites
- **Stocks and materials** – loss, damage or theft of stock
- **Legal expenses** – covers legal expenses or fees for things like employment tribunals or HMRC tax investigations

Commercial contracts

Your new business will have contracts to both buy and sell goods or services, which are controlled by contract law.

What is a contract?

A contract is a legally binding agreement between at least two parties. The basic principles of forming a contract govern formation of all contracts to:

- Obtain services
- Sell a product
- Sell a business
- Buy IP
- Sell products to consumers
- Give a guarantee

Essential elements of contracts

Five elements must be satisfied to have a contract exist:

1. One party makes an offer ('Offer')
2. The other party accepts the offer ('Acceptance')
3. One party provides consideration to the other Consideration (which can be as small as £1) can be:
    a. a promise to pay money
    b. a promise to do something
    c. a promise not to do something, or
    d. promise to provide something else of value
4. Intention to be legally bound: both parties have an intention to be legally bound by the agreement (which is proposed by the offer, and then accepted)
5. The parties have contractual capacity: the parties are legal entities recognised by law, such as companies, or individuals of at least 18 years of age

Contracts can be verbal or in writing.

Contracts can be binding without being written down.

What contracts do I need?

This book cannot offer legal advice. Many sectors have their own ways of working, and contracts to suit. Fortunately, much information is available online.

Terms and Conditions (Ts & Cs)

When you enter into a contract with a customer, you will normally do it under your Ts & Cs. It is important that you have Ts & Cs, and that the customer is fully aware of what they are. The Ts & Cs will include such things as terms of payment, guarantees, returns, and dispute resolution.

It is worth checking out what Ts & Cs your competition is using and look at their standard terms, which you can find online, as this will help inform your own approach.

Ts & Cs are a complex area but try not to reinvent the wheel and use a model that works well already. There are many templates available, by business type, online.

It is very important to seek advice.

Use your own strong contract

Having strong contract terms and conditions that your customers are aware of is a great benefit, as both parties clearly know where they stand if something goes wrong. This will include your own terms and conditions.

What about intellectual property (IP)?

We talked in Chapter 26 about IP. All IP used should be properly registered, and protected, if appropriate.

If a business is trying to develop a specialist niche, the entrepreneurs may personally develop tools, software, techniques or ideas that can be classed as their own IP.

Most employment contracts for employees will automatically pass any IP generated by an employee to the employer. That is fair enough for employers, as they take all the commercial risks on behalf of that employee and guarantee to indemnify employees against third parties.

It therefore makes sense that if a business generates or brings IP to a project, that the IP remains the property of the business, but the customer can use it with permission.

I covered this element in my own contracts by ensuring that my company was recognised as the owner of any IP used or generated in the project, and that the customer was granted a lifetime licence to use that IP.

Be sure that using any IP you may hold is protected contractually so that customers cannot use it inappropriately.

Secret No. 29 Clear contracts help all parties avoid disputes, protect IP and ensure commitment

Next Action: Learn about contracts so you can use them for your new business' benefit

Chapter 29 Ownership of the business – key percentages of voting shares

What percentage of shares should you hold in a limited company?

Your percentage shareholding in a private limited company is subject to several rules. Key thresholds dictate how much power a shareholder has in running a company.

If you plan to run a solo business, then this is not an issue. For those thinking about business partners, these voting share percentages should be considered:

Limited company: hierarchy of ownership overview

Percentage Shareholding	Rights
100%	Can do anything
90%	Hold General Meeting at short notice
75%	Pass Special Resolution (e.g. change name, articles, force winding up)
50+%	Pass any item of routine business etc
25%+	Block a Special Resolution
10%	Right to have company's accounts audited

100% is really the 'holy grail' of ownership, with the shareholder able to do anything. Solo businesses can benefit from this position easily.

75% is a powerful percentage to hold, as you can pass special resolutions. You can also incentivise team members or staff with the remaining shares or options if needed.

Over 50%, you can pass routine business, but require another 25% to vote to pass special resolutions (which can fundamentally change the business).

Under 50% the rights are limited.

Beware 50:50 share splits

On the face of it, a 50:50 split between two partners sounds very fair and equitable. I would advise caution.

I have come across companies owned 50:50 from the outset, as the directors regarded themselves as equal partners. This can sometimes lead to total gridlock if the shareholders disagree on a particular course of action.

This happened to one client, when one shareholder was active running the business and wanted to take an approach that would help the business survive. The passive 50% shareholder would not budge. It was a very expensive situation to resolve.

You could have a 50:50 shareholder split by having a separate shareholder agreement with an agreed and specified form of dispute resolution, but is it worth it?

Final thoughts on shareholdings

Only give away voting equity as a last resort and think carefully about the percentages held.

Secret No. 30 Think very carefully about the percentages of voting shares given to the founding team to avoid control problems later on

Next Action: Learn about the different rights attaching to different percentages of shares in limited companies

Chapter 30 How to win at finance

A bank is a place where they lend you an umbrella in fair weather and ask for it back when it begins to rain.

Robert Frost –American Poet.

This chapter is about managing finance in a positive way and managing a way through cash challenges, which are an inevitable part of running a business.

What is cashflow?

Cash flow is the net amount of cash and cash-equivalents being transferred into and out of a business. (Investopedia)

Every business and person has a cash flow. Income comes in, and outgoings go out, and the balance is 'positive cash flow' or 'negative cash flow'.

Money makes the world (and your business) go around

Cash flow challenges are inevitable for any new business. As we saw at the beginning of the book, most business failures are due to a lack of cash.

Positive cash flow is fantastic, if your business can achieve it. Conversely long-term negative cash flow can affect the business substantially, as management time is taken up with trying to improve cash flow rather than growing the business.

Secret No. 31 Cash is king – it really is!

Next Action: Prepare an accurate cash flow to make sure you generate the cash required to run the business

There is more detail about cash and optimising cash flow in Chapter 39 and Chapter 50.

Cash needs active management

Many people probably has some personal experience of having a tight cashflow at the end of the month before the wages or salary gets cleared through the bank. Cash needs actively managing, with action taken to rectify adverse trends.

Do the sums properly on a spreadsheet

Using a spreadsheet, like Excel (Microsoft) or Numbers (Apple), is a major benefit for controlling your cashflow.

I have included a simple cash flow outline, that you can easily tailor to your own requirements, and for as many periods as you need, by adding extra rows or columns.

The good thing about spreadsheets is that they are very accurate if you 'prove' them 'right', as in the example with small trial numbers. Be careful though, and always double check the output for any 'finger trouble' that may have accidently altered formulae or input numbers.

Mistakes on spreadsheets can be the source of major embarrassment and even business failure.

Use a simple cashflow model

	Simple Cash Flow Model			
		Month 1	Month 2	Month 3
Cash In	Sales	-	10	20
	Capital	100	-	-
	Other	-	-	-
	Total	**100**	**10**	**20**
Cash Out	Suppliers	-	5	10
	Overheads	20	20	20
	Salaries	10	10	10
	PAYE	-	1	1
	VAT	-	-	-
	Other	-	-	-
	Total	**30**	**36**	**41**
Net		**70**	**(26)**	**(21)**
Bank Balance	Opening	-	70	44
	Closing	70	44	23

Using a model like this starts a learning process about cash flow.

In business, a lot of the outgoing cash numbers are relatively fixed (e.g. overheads and salaries), with the unknowns being the level of sales, and the cash being banked from sales. As time goes on, you can develop assumptions about when you will be paid, such as how many days customers will take to pay. It helps to write the assumptions down at the bottom of the spreadsheet.

Judgement and knowledge about this important area improves with experience of the business and running spreadsheets like this. It always helps to have someone else check out the numbers and your assumptions for validity.

To help, here are the formulae for the spreadsheet:

1	B	C	D	E	F
2		Simple Cash Flow Model			
3					
4			Month 1	Month 2	Month 3
5					
6	**Cash In**	Sales	0	10	20
7		Capital	100	0	0
8		Other	0	0	0
9					
10		**Total**	**=SUM(D6:D9)**	**=SUM(E6:E9)**	**=SUM(F6:F9)**
11					
12	**Cash Out**	Suppliers	0	5	10
13		Overheads	20	20	20
14		Salaries	10	10	10
15		PAYE	0	1	1
16		VAT	0	0	0
17		Other	0	0	0
18					
19		**Total**	**=SUM(D12:D18**	**=SUM(E12:E18)**	**=SUM(F12:F18)**
20					
21	**Net**		**=D10-D19**	**=E10-E19**	**=F10-F19**
22					
23	**Bank Balance**	Opening	0	=D24	=E24
24		Closing	=D23+D21	=E23+E21	=F23+F21

You can modify this format to cover days, months or weeks if required.

Run a weekly cashflow if you need to

I once worked in a company so short of cash, its major focus was on the cash due in that week, to pay the weekly wages on the Friday. The priority was the weekly cash flow, backed up by a three-monthly view. I am glad to say, that the Finance Director of this company always paid my wages on the Friday, so his weekly cash flow plans worked.

How much money does the business need?

Using these tools, you can establish your first view of how much money the business will need to meet its start-up milestones. The optimum idea is to minimise external sources of funding to keep the start-up simple.

Is there a 'holy grail' of start-ups?

Take the optimum route for a business start-up if you can:

- Start with little capital (say £100)
- Generate cash from day one
- Have no borrowings
- Grow profitability and cash flow organically with no financing

My guess is that this scenario is a pretty rare beast, but as an ideal, it is worth striving for. The complexity and length of time that raising money adds to a start-up affects its opportunity to win business in the short term.

Capital input from shareholders

Clearly if finance is required, it is up to the shareholders to find it, either from their own pockets or externally. There are many types of finance available.

Types of finance available to start-ups

Individuals can use personal finance products to lend to their business, such as:

- Credit cards
- Overdraft
- Bank loans
- Family loans
- Second mortgage
- Inheritance
- Borrowings from relatives
- Start-up loans and funding

Business finance is available to the business directly:

- Capital input from founders/investors
- Bank overdraft
- Bank term loans
- Asset finance (factoring, hire purchase, leasing)

How much finance is needed?

This is literally the $64,000 question. Invariably the answer will be much more than planned.

The level required clearly depends on many factors, such as the type of business, how much capital needs to be raised, and whether several shareholders are involved.

If you have produced a cashflow for the business as part of the business plan, you will have some idea of the scale of cash raising required. The sums that your cash flow produce depend on the assumptions you have used. What if those assumptions are too optimistic?

Be very, very conservative

Being overly optimistic has the potential to kill a business stone dead. Everything in practice usually takes a lot longer than you initially think. Winning the first contract, setting up a website, moving into a new factory or office etc. can all take more time than you planned for. This may be for many different reasons (this is where the **unknown unknowns** can cause major damage).

Always use a contingency

Think about adding in contingencies to your calculations to offset some of these unknown factors. It will add credibility to your plan.

Security for borrowings

As bank lending to businesses changes and products offered change rapidly over time, it is impossible to recommend specific products.

In theory, aim to borrow little externally, with no security (i.e. business loans are unsecured).

If it is impossible to raise commercial finance for your business, think about using personal borrowings if you have to, provided that you are confident that you will be repaid from the business in due course.

Always take the best advice if you must give any security for business borrowings. Local business financial advice may well be available through your local business advisory centre.

Secret No. 32 A conservative cash flow with known assumptions, and a contingency to cover 'unknown unknowns' makes sense

Next Action: Plan your cashflow using a spreadsheet, but be very conservative

Chapter 31 How much should I charge?

The moment you make a mistake in pricing, you're eating into your reputation or your profits.

Katharine Paine – Chief Marketing Officer, News Group

Pricing is critical

Pricing is the most critical component in order to maximise your sales revenue and profits.

In the USA, Harvard studies have found that a 1% improvement in pricing can add up to 11% to your profits. With bad pricing, you are missing out on profits in every transaction you make, plus the deals that you miss out on.

Reducing prices is easier than increasing prices

Pricing is also a big factor in your business' branding and reputation. Prices set too high can make your business seem remote from the market, while prices set too low can call the quality of your products or services into question. Reducing prices, although easy in principle, can have a very adverse effect on the profitability and viability of the business

Is it easier to charge too little?

If you are thinking of running a service business, and effectively charging by the hour, it is relatively easy to fall into the trap of undercutting market rates to win business volume. This creates a problem that may be difficult to solve, particularly if you cannot make enough money to maintain your lifestyle. It could be very challenging to have to increase prices substantially after a business launch.

How much should I charge?

Clearly, prices will vary depending on whether your business sells time, services or products. Each business will operate in a market where certain prices are generally accepted. A haircut costs £x, a plumber's day rate is £y and a consultancy day rate is £z. Remember, though, that in the consultancy market, people are paying a premium price that is also buying 20 years of experience.

The same pricing principles apply to products, such as a bakery producing loaves of bread.

We operate in a capitalist free market, so a business can normally charge what it likes. However, the economic laws of supply and demand apply 99% of the time, which normally self-regulate prices.

Commodity versus 'added value' pricing

What is a commodity?

A commodity is a basic good used in commerce that is interchangeable with other goods of the same type. Commodities are most often used as inputs in the production of other goods or services. The quality of a given commodity may differ slightly, but it is essentially uniform across producers.

Investopedia

Loaves of bread

Think about the example of a loaf of bread. At the time of writing there is a substantial difference in pricing between different types of bread from different retail suppliers:

Soft white sliced	Aldi	£0.49
White medium sliced	Tesco	£0.59
Kingsmill Medium Sliced	Sainsbury	£1.00
Farmhouse Batch	Waitrose	£1.45
Organic Seeded Sliced Bloomer	Waitrose	£1.85
48-hour Sourdough	Independent	£3.50

There is a rough difference in price of 7.1 times between the lowest and highest prices in this example – you may find bigger differences locally.

Which are volume commodity products?

The first two products are the big volume 'commodity' loaves that sell on price alone.

Think about the pricing challenge that Aldi and its supplier have. They want to deliver the lowest price per loaf (cheaper than 50p), while making profit and not degrading product quality. This is a major challenge and can sometimes be a 'race to the bottom' where the supplier cannot make money from producing bread but cannot afford to lose the Aldi contract because it is so large.

For a new entrant to be active in this market, a bakery needs to produce enough volume at the lowest possible viable cost to satisfy a major supermarket chain. That would require a huge multi-million-pound investment and overcoming major barriers to entry (e.g. winning the Aldi contract away from the current supplier).

Brands and added value

Above the £0.60 per loaf price, other factors come into play, such as brand (Kingsmill or Waitrose) or added value content such as ingredient quality.

Bespoke, handmade, organic ingredients

Above £2 per loaf, the products move away from commodity to smaller batch products. Over £3 they are likely to be small batch, or handmade from top quality ingredients.

How bread products are different

Market Volume	High	Medium	Low
Products	Commodity	Branded	Niche, bespoke
Price	Lowest – nearly fixed	Medium	Higher – more flexible
Competition	High	High	High
Capital cost of start-up	High	High?	Low?
Start-up opportunity	Disrupt	Disrupt	Compete

In what sector of the market will your business compete?

Are you in a commodity market, or can you command a special price for added value? You can research prices or market rates fairly easily through the internet, and also by talking to contacts in the business.

Niche market pricing is less competitive

Try to find a unique product or service, or market niche, where price is less important than the quality or other USPs of the product or service.

Find a price bracket for your new business you are comfortable with

You can then get a price bracket you are comfortable with, and then look at your personal and potential business cost base (the level of income you need to cover your costs). The question of how much money you need to make to pay the bills has to be answered, and how much income is sacrificed while the business gets going.

External factors affecting pricing

Market rates

Research, knowledge, and preparation are the real keys here, and recognition of where the real business value lies. The top market rates go to those businesses with the best propositions and track records, or in limited niche markets or market sectors, where customers are prepared to pay more for a special product or service.

Don't be embarrassed talking about money

Generally, you have to face up to a customer and say what the product or service costs. There can be a particularly British cultural issue to deal with here; some people may have difficulty talking about money or negotiating directly when it affects them personally. It would be difficult to run a business if they could not change their behaviour.

Working or selling for lower prices than normal

When market conditions are strong, there should only be rare occasions where a business needs to consider working at below normal rates. When times are tough, however, it may be necessary to take on work just to generate cash flow for the business.

Follow the money

My approach to this position is that a business 'has to do what it has to do' to keep the show on the road. Remember that the 'bird in the hand' is very strong, particularly when it adds to positive cash flow. At times like this 'follow the money'.

Pitching your price in a 'sealed bid' competition

A business may be asked to bid for work in a 'sealed bid' or blind situation where there is no budget or indication of pricing. Glean as much intelligence as possible about the customer and its business before pitching. Also, discover who else is bidding, although this may be difficult.

My view would be to bid at normal market rate plus or minus a small amount to recognise current market conditions. Take account of your business' own potential for other work in the pipeline and stress the reasons you are the right supplier for the project. If the business has other firm prospects in the pipeline, you may want to bid over, or around your normal rate, depending on how interesting the order looks.

Chapter 32 How do I work out my costs?

Watch the costs and the profits will take care of themselves.

Andrew Carnegie – US Industrialist

Fixing day rates

Day rates for many businesses are an important, subtle and complex area. They must be dealt with on a satisfactory basis for both the business and the customer.

With the right approach to rates, a business might win more sales, or make enough money for their business to succeed. It is vital to get this right, or as 'right as possible' to the satisfaction of all the parties.

Experience, market intelligence and preparation help enormously. A realistic assessment and proper recognition of a business's price position in the market, and product offering is vital. Achieving a good price is the potential difference between business success and failure.

Taking a professional approach and separating the emotional element also helps. In terms of day rates, people generally like to think that they are worth more than they perhaps are. Selling time in a business is an exercise in pragmatism and realism, although this can conflict with a desire not to be too big-headed or to undercharge. Balance is everything, and this is sometimes challenging to achieve.

How do day rates relate to salaries?

Earning a salary is straightforward. There is gross pay and take-home pay, with deductions such as national insurance (NI), pension and tax. The employment position has a known notice period if it is terminated.

Understanding the mechanism of how gross salaries relate to day rates is important for the success of a business, but there are technicalities to cover.

What are the total costs of employing someone?

It is useful to understand the numbers for establishing a daily charge-out rate. The average UK salary in 2019 was £36,611 (Office of National Statistics).

Assuming a salary near the average of £40,000 (and minimal employee benefits except pension and life assurance), how much does it cost an employer?

This estimate excludes recruitment, business overheads, software, consumables, and travel.

Estimated total costs of employment

Item	Cost £
Salary	40,000
National Insurance – employer's contribution	3,764
Pension (say 10%)	4,000
Total Cost	47,764
	Days
UK workdays in a year (52 x 5)	260
Holidays (say 25 + 8 statutory)	-33
Training	-5
Days Sick, say	-7
Total days available	215
	Cost £
Cost per day	£222.15

Without overheads (which would usually be a substantial add-on), the headline daily rate for an equivalent £40k salary works out at £222.15.

Baker Ali needs to know about costs

Let us assume that a baker, Ali, wants to set up a solo mini-bakery and is interested in a costing for the business.

Ali has been lucky to rent an equipped bakery for 12 months and has a contact on a local market who can sell 1,000 loaves a week, based on a £3 retail selling price, and £1.50 wholesale price.

What are the costs to consider?

Costs generally come in two sorts:

- Direct costs
- Indirect costs (or overheads)

Direct costs are those which are directly related to a particular job or product. For a baker, this would be flour, water, yeast, other materials and power for the oven. These are Ali's direct costs:

Gross Margin	**£ Per loaf**
Selling Price	1.50
Material costs & power	0.25
Gross margin per loaf	1.25

Ali's indirect costs are overheads, which include rent, telephone, accountancy and so on.

Here is Ali's estimate of costs:

Ali's Cost Estimate

	Per Year	Per Month
Indirect Costs	£	
Ali's Salary	47,764	3,980
Phone	600	50
Rent	12,000	1,000
Accountancy	1,000	83
Insurance	500	42
Legal	500	42
Other	1,636	136
Total	**64,000**	**5,333**

Will Ali make a profit selling 1,000 loaves a week?

Profit & Loss				
	Per Month	**Per Month**	**Per Month**	**Per Month**
Number of loaves	3,000	4,000	4,250	5,000
Sales value	4,500	6,000	6,375	7,500
Direct Material costs	750	1,000	1,063	1,250
Gross margin	3,750	5,000	5,313	6,250
Overheads	5,333	5,333	5,333	5,333
Profit/(loss)	(1,583)	(333)	(21)	917

Ali's customer at the market can only sell 1,000 loaves a week, totalling 4,000 a month, so Ali will lose £333 per month, unless other customers can be found for the remaining capacity of 250 loaves per week.

Ali is very fortunate that the gross profit made on each extra loaf is substantial (£1.25). If production capacity can be expanded at little cost, and the extra output sold, Ali should be able to build a highly profitable business.

As an example of success, the baker that supplies my local market stall with high quality bread, now supplies over 50 markets in the South of England every week and has built up a substantial business.

Deriving a day or hourly rate

A business can calculate the salary level, and an 'employed daily rate' from the tools above and look at their own personal financial requirements. (Be careful to check exact costs for your expected salary and benefits.)

Having looked at the marketplace, and a business' personal requirements, the owner should be able to calculate a 'top-level' and 'bottom level' day rate that suits their own business circumstances and personal financial requirements. The challenge is to find and secure work within those rates.

Secret No. 33 Know your business numbers, and where you can improve profitability without increasing your cost base

Next Action: If volume is important, build a simple spreadsheet of the impact of volume sales on your business

Chapter 33 Optimising the transition and making the leap

Jump, and you will find out how to unfold your wings as you fall.

Ray Bradbury – US Author

Making a big life change is pretty scary. But, know what's even scarier? Regret.

Anonymous

Two quotes

I have purposely used the two quotes to show the tensions (the 'shall I, shan't I?' decision) at the moment that a new business is launched.

This chapter is about optimising the transition and making sure that it goes smoothly.

What should you have done before starting your business?

In terms of starting a business, many things need to be completed, or be ready to complete before the business can start.

Like Baker Ali in the previous chapter, you will have done all the sums, and produced a clear business plan and cash flow appropriate to the business you wish to start.

What needs to be ready, and up and running, to start a business?

Here is a list of many items in no particular order. You may also have other specific things to add for your business:

- Approvals, licences, permits and certifications and Brexit impact
- Trading vehicle and structure in place
- A business name or company name
- Trading address
- Register with HMRC for PAYE and VAT (if appropriate)
- Bank account
- Finance in place
- Legally allowed to trade
- Prospect of orders and revenue
- Ability to supply customers
- Insurances
- Personal data and information rules
- Website
- Bookkeeping and invoicing system
- IP – trademarks and patents
- Writing and testing bespoke software
- Off-the-shelf software
- Computer equipment/phones
- Production or supply chain in place

Looking at this list of items, I have categorised them into three sections to show what can generally be done in advance, and what takes money or time. The table shows my opinions and experience – your list may be different. The items have then been put in order to see if they can be done in advance or not.

What can be done in advance of business launch?

	Can be done in advance?*	Takes time?*	Takes money?*
Trading vehicle and structure in place, Brexit impact	Yes	Yes	Little
Approvals, licences, permits and certifications	Yes	Yes	?
Business name	Yes	No	No
Trading address	Yes	?	?
Register with HMRC	Yes	No	No
Bank account	Yes	Yes	Yes
Insurance	Yes	?	Yes
Data and information rules	Yes	?	?
Website	Yes	Yes	?
Bookkeeping and invoice system	Yes	?	Yes
Off-the-shelf software	Yes	No	Yes
Computer equipment/phones	Yes	No	Yes
Legally allowed to trade	?	?	No
Prospect of orders and revenue	?	Yes	Yes
Ability to supply customers	?	Yes	Yes
Production or supply chain in place	?	Yes	Yes
Finance in place	?	?	?
IP	?	Yes	Yes
Writing bespoke software	?	Yes	Yes

**My view – actual practice may differ* [italic]

Have as much ready as possible

The trick here is to have as much ready as possible before a launch.

Any time spent doing set-up work after launch is time lost on winning new orders or expanding the business.

Secret No. 34 Have as much of the set-up done as possible before you launch. This gives more time to grow the business at its most vulnerable stage

Next Action: Prepare and complete your own set-up list before launch

Part 6 – Launch – 'We have ignition'

Chapter 34 Creating the winning mindset

If my mind can conceive it and my heart can believe it – then I can achieve it.

Mohammed Ali – Champion professional boxer and activist

The winning mindset

What is the winning mindset needed to build a business, and how can it be developed and nurtured?

It takes time to fully develop the mindset, but by making the right start, you can then take pleasure in small steps and triumphs. Building on a good positive start is important, which is why the time spent on planning is so valuable.

Small steps create momentum

Starting a business that is well prepared, well planned and well thought-through will instil confidence, particularly if you have had external positive feedback for your plans. A winning mindset grows from a dream, idea or vision, and builds on that foundation. It will grow by small, but significant early steps through confident action.

Grit: perseverance and passion

Grit is needed. Professor Angela Duckworth (University of Pennsylvania) defines grit as the combination of passion and perseverance for a unique, long-term goal. She argues that the ability to rebound from adversity and maintain focus is the greatest contributor to business success. She believes that you can measure and then improve your grit, which is separate from other talents the entrepreneur may have. There is more on this in Chapter 43.

Stay with the vision

Belief and commitment to the vision are essential and having a long-term view and confidence in that belief. Grit and determination are a large part of this process, but pragmatism, being realistic and prepared to adapt the vision as the knowledge base grows are acceptable.

Actions speak louder than words

Running a business is about making decisions, often without access to the full facts. Not making a decision may be an easy (and, possibly, usual) option for a bureaucrat, but generally, it is not an option for an entrepreneur. Realise that there are the 'quick and the dead', and that speed is generally important in a highly competitive and quickly changing environment.

Believe it in your heart

Grow the vision and develop your business ethos and culture from a one-person or partnership small start to a multinational organisation.

There is more on mindset and the Coronavirus in Part 9.

Secret No. 35 Develop the winning mindset

Next Action: Be positive about every setback and believe that it can be done. Find solutions

Chapter 35 How do I win business?

You were born to win, but to be a winner, you must plan to win, prepare to win, and expect to win.

Zig Zigler – US Author

So, where do you start?

New businesses must sell or generate income to stay in business, but marketing, selling and closing deals are not necessarily the 'natural' business of a new entrepreneur. So, a new business must grapple with this potentially 'unnatural' sales and marketing activity to win business, which must take place on a regular and sometimes highly intensive basis.

Those entrepreneurs starting a business with a sales or marketing background often have a great advantage in being able to 'hit the ground running'.

What is the difference between marketing and selling?

To sell something, a business must have a customer first, and a product or service to sell. Marketing identifies the customer, and what the customer wants.

The sales process then follows on from that by pitching to the customer and closing the proposition to obtain orders. My view of this process, and how different activities take place in the sales or marketing stream is outlined below.

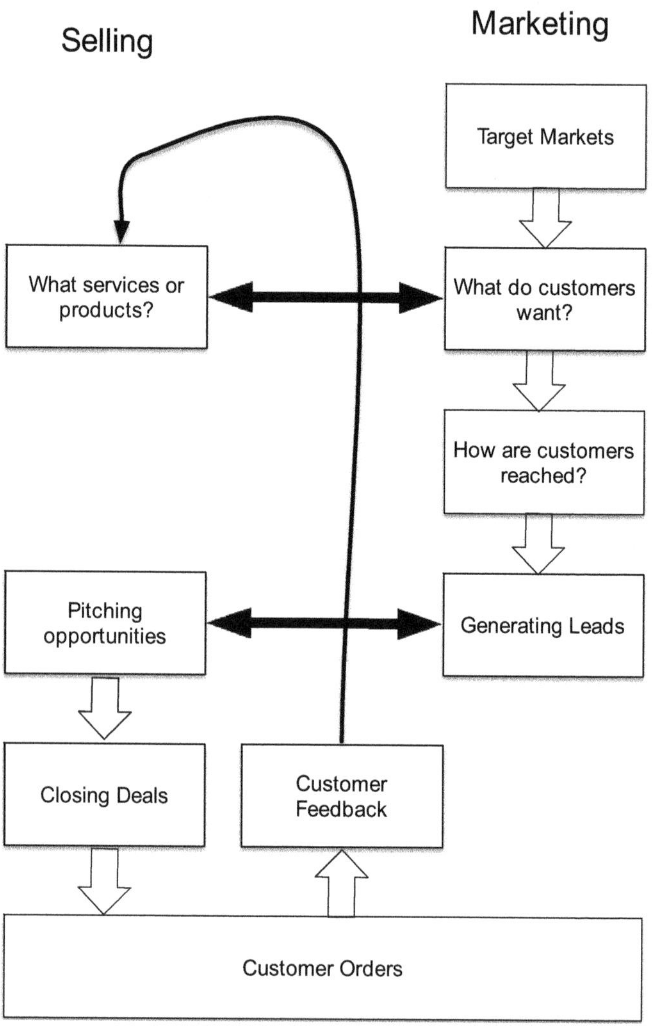

This process can take place on a face-to-face basis, by email and post, and also online.

The feedback loop is an important part of this whole process, as it enables the business to recalibrate its product or service offering or pricing, dependant on the feedback received.

Marketing is about effective activity

Marketing takes a finite amount of time and has several discrete steps. We have seen that to maintain a good flow of orders, there will be sporadic peaks of high marketing activity. There will also be regular marketing maintenance activity continuing on a planned basis to keep customer options open. A small business requires significant discipline to maintain this regular level of required marketing activity while delivering products or services for customers.

Marketing channels

There are an increasing multitude of channels through which to reach potential customers, including social media.

Whichever channels are chosen to use to get the message across to potential customers, marketing is about effective activity and discipline.

Online and retail marketing

Retail or internet businesses will have different approaches, such as seasonal marketing campaigns. They will also collect a lot of data about which campaigns are most effective and when.

Measure success rates across channels

Measure the success rates of each channel and type of activity so the business can discover what works best. A business may end up with a portfolio within which they have a few, highly targeted activities.

Use Customer Relationship Management (CRM) tools

CRM refers to practices and technologies that manage and analyse customer interactions throughout the customer lifecycle. The goal is to improve business relationships with customers, assisting in customer retention and driving out more business. CRM systems help businesses develop prospects into customers by providing an efficient route in managing and storing information on leads and contacts.

The purpose of a CRM system is to attract and retain customers, and works by logging all contacts with them, providing useful data on what works. There are many systems available, both for mobile devices and PC's. Online businesses will have their own CRM analysis.

Consistently following up leads and monitoring them can be very useful. In my business, I found simple CRM tools useful to ensure that I was on top of all the marketing activity needed and could measure the impact of different approaches.

Some Ideas for Marketing Strategies

Opportunity cost or opportunity income?

When selling time, such as consultancy, for example, sitting at home at down times is a costly option, unless taking a break has been planned. Avoid a project finishing at the end of June, as marketing and closing a deal during July or August normally has the odds stacked against it. An enforced break of eight weeks in the summer is generally to be avoided, unless it has been planned. That enforced break will burn up cash reserves, and the opportunity cost can be high.

Learn and follow the annual cycle

There may be a perception that businesses will work all year, as employees do. This is not normally a problem as far as delivering the work or product is concerned, but for getting orders, an annual cycle is often likely to apply. It is therefore essential to be strategic about the timing of marketing and closing business deals.

Does seasonality apply?

Think about the cycles that typical seasonal products face, like the popular example of selling ice cream mainly in the summer, or umbrellas mainly in the winter. Plumbers, for example are very busy in the winter as boilers and heating systems fail, and less busy in the summer.

Allocate activity to certain parts of the year

Sometimes, it is useful to split the year up like a school year into three terms: Spring, Summer and Autumn. The intervening periods during the Easter, Summer and Christmas holidays are slower for both activity and decision-making in organisations.

In the public sector particularly, this aspect is more pronounced as civil servants not only have considerable holiday entitlements, but they also get privilege days (extra holidays) like Maundy Thursday before Good Friday at Easter. Marketing to the public sector just before Easter can be very counterproductive.

Find the marketing 'good times'

Often, good times for marketing activity peak during September, January and April. Having said this there will always be a few urgent exceptions that disprove the rule. Other times risk being a lot less productive, and some months, like July and August can be positively difficult for getting orders. Spring can also be a challenging time as there are so many bank holidays.

Optimising the timing of these cycles can be very productive and can enhance total annual sales, if the timing and planning of activity is right.

Maximising annual days worked

When selling time or consultancy, customers always seem to want a quick start, and being able to 'start next Monday' not only helps get a new project off on the right foot, but also helps close the deal.

Managing workflow

It is often difficult to influence the start date of a project, as both the consultant and the customer will usually want to start soon. This helps both to generate cash for the business, and to get the show on the road for the customer. The same is true in other businesses, but there may be more of an issue in weaving the new work into an existing workplan. Many trades have traditionally been very opaque about the timing for 'starting work' and thereby lose a lot of goodwill.

Taking breaks and holidays

In my consultancy business, I found it was often better to take time off within a contract, if the timetable of the project and its deliverables were not affected. If a consultant is working on a longer-term project, of, say over six months, it will be seen by the customer as reasonable to take holidays (as all their other employees do). But remember that for a consultant, the holiday is unpaid, and this provides a challenge in terms of accumulating funds to pay for that time off. Holidays have a finite opportunity cost.

Marketing can be done while working on a contract, whereas taking a break when a project ends means that marketing will impinge on the holiday with possible negative effects, as the marketing may not be done properly and in good time. There is a danger that not enough time is spent on marketing for the next piece of work, while taking a break.

Taking breaks within a contract also leaves a consultant clear to market and to take on the next project straight afterwards.

What are my target markets?

My preference is for a well thought-through marketing strategy tightly targeted to a small range of well vetted prospects; the 'rifle shot', rather than the looser 'scatter gun' approach.

It is about focus, and using time spent in marketing effectively. For a one-person business to succeed, the effective use of time, concentrated on those potential leads that will deliver business, is essential.

Use serendipity to your advantage

There is a powerful luck or serendipity in this marketing process, particularly at start-up.

Serendipity is *the occurrence and development of events by chance in a happy or beneficial way (Oxford Dictionaries).*

A new entrepreneur will deal across all their existing network and contacts. They will come across opportunities and ideas that arise from their various discussions across that range of contacts. I think they may be pleasantly surprised how many opportunities can arise if their net is spread wide enough.

Reaching the right decision makers

When operating in a niche product market or specialist consultancy there may only be, say 200 to 300 decision makers that control the work in a particular market network who need to be influenced.

Identifying them is one thing: getting the right messages across at the right time requires a great deal more expertise. Those 300 decision makers will not necessarily all have a business need for services or new products right now. What is important is that the decision maker knows who the entrepreneur is, and when the need arises, they know who to call.

Market research

Part of the business plan should include some basic market research questions that need to be answered:

- What is the current demand in those markets that the entrepreneur decides are appropriate, and what are the prices that the market will pay?
- Who is in the entrepreneur's existing set of contacts and network?

- Who are the business' potential target customers?
- Which potential customer is most likely to give the business orders?

The marketing funnel

Marketing is a distinct process that takes time and resources to undertake properly. It works like a funnel attached to the top of the business' pipeline of work.

The breadth of the funnel, and the number of potential prospects put in at the top will dictate the success in getting business into the pipeline, and the level of sales.

An entrepreneur will need to clearly understand what methods of marketing work for them and their market, and what level of activity they need to reach to close a deal. This means keeping the funnel topped up with enough prospects to ensure that sufficient business is generated from deals that have been closed.

Think of the funnel as constantly flowing – if the prospects have run through already, it will need topping up.

Marketing response rates

An illustration of the marketing funnel and the more 'scattergun' approach is shown by direct marketing such as mailshots and leafleting.

In my experience, before data protection regulations, a niche market mailshot yielded around 5% responses (such as 'we'll keep you on file') with perhaps 1% usable as qualified, convertible leads. So, the funnel generates say, 1 prospect per hundred mailshots. By comparison, mainstream direct mail houses claim around 3.5% success rate across the general population in a retail type environment. Note that General Data Protection

Regulations (GDPR) are applicable for data protection for unsolicited emails.

Other funnel inputs

The marketing funnel has many more inputs of different technologies, such as LinkedIn, Twitter, internet sites, email, online tools, and some of the older methods like telesales and direct mail. All marketing activities will have their own success ratios that it is helpful to learn and understand.

Conversion rates of prospects

The 1% response rate to mail above illustrates that different activities will have different response rates. The ultimate question is how much activity is needed across the whole marketing spectrum with different response rates to meet the business' targets. With this knowledge, and being forearmed, the level of required activity across all channels becomes self-evident to secure a sustainable level of business.

Use of external marketing consultants

Some businesses start where the founders have little or no sales and marketing experience. Consider getting help from external consultants if you are in this position. Sales and marketing can be a severe stumbling block for new businesses that focus narrowly on product or service delivery.

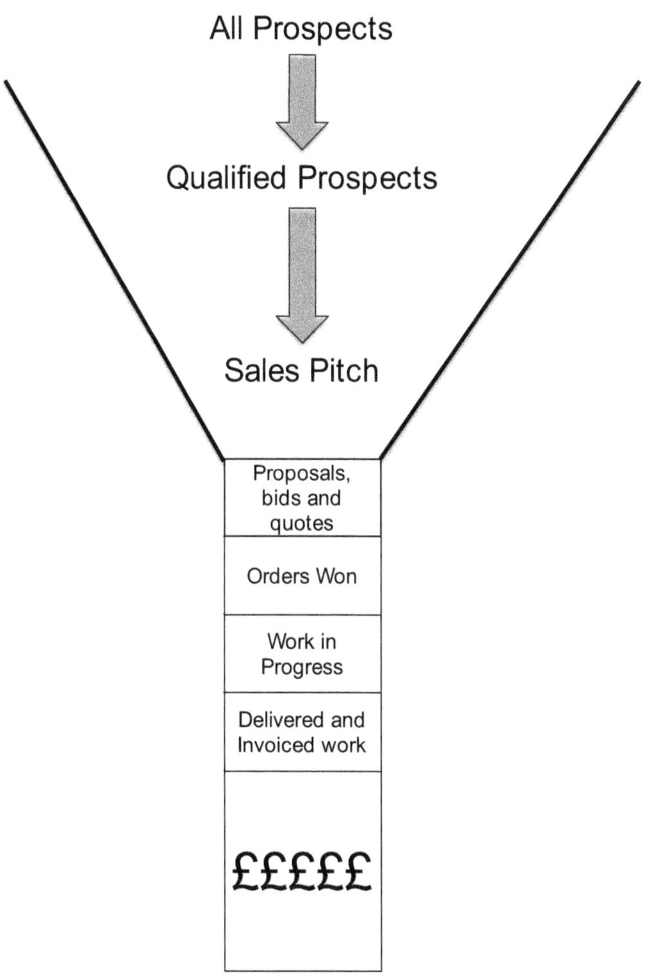
The Marketing Funnel
All Prospects
Qualified Prospects
Sales Pitch
Proposals, bids and quotes
Orders Won
Work in Progress
Delivered and Invoiced work
£££££

A typical pattern

If we assume that we have a 1% conversion rate from all marketing activity, and need 4 orders per month to run the business properly, the sums would be as follows per year:

Marketing activity	4,800
Converted orders	48

The lesson here is that the marketing activity required is high, if conversion rates are low. This will clearly depend on the business, and the marketing channnels used.

If you can find a more efficient way of converting leads, let's say a 10% conversion rate, up from 1%, the numbers are much more encouraging:

Marketing activity	480
Converted orders	48

This can be a process of trial and error to find the right way to approach customers. The rewards can be substantial once the right solutions are found.

Secret No. 36 The right level of marketing activity will bring dividends

Next Action: Do the sums for your planned marketing activity, working on conservative conversion rates to bring in the number of leads the business needs

Chapter 36 The front office – marketing and selling

The front office represents the customer-facing function of a firm, for example, customer service, sales, and industry experts who provide advisory services. The functions of the front office generate most of the revenue for the firm. Many firms can be divided into two parts, the front office performing sales and client service functions, and the back office, which provides analysis, technical, and administrative support services.

Investopedia

Organising your business

The front office deals with customer-facing activity, and business generation while the back office deals with administration and accounting. A new entrepreneur will often work on their own, so must get used to dealing with all these functions until the business is large enough to have separate departments. Think about your business having a customer-facing front office, for sales and marketing and an administrative back office.

The marketing challenge

As we have seen in the previous chapter, some marketing techniques deliver low levels of opportunity that require high levels of activity. Find efficient ways of marketing a business, particularly with new technology, that can be productive.

Low frequency or continuous marketing?

Marketing can fall into two approaches, depending on the product or service:

- Low frequency marketing for high value products
- High frequency or continuous marketing for low value and repeat purchase products

It is worth considering, early in the business planning stage, exactly how an efficient marketing operation will work to develop a viable business.

There are many ways of approaching this issue, and new inventive approaches may well work.

Part of the benefit of using CRM tools is to establish what methods work best, and why. This can be a process of trial and error, and may change radically over time, as business and economic circumstances change.

Different routes to market

Some routes to market are outlined below (this is not an exhaustive list):

Marketing to the personal network

From the outset establish:

- Which markets are the focus?
- Where geographically are these markets based?
- What channels will approach these markets?
- Who are the individuals to be targeted?

As we have seen before, if, say, a new consultant is working in a niche with 100 potential clients in that niche, normally only a small percentage of them may have a demand for the entrepreneur's expertise at any one time. This is where market intelligence comes in, and the discussions with both their own network and other contacts can point to opportunities in specific organisations, as and when they develop.

Leveraging the network

How can an entrepreneur leverage their existing network to get business in their main sector and possibly in other sectors? This is where entrepreneurialism comes in. With imagination and creativity (and a little luck), good solutions can often be found.

Indirect methods work well

I am a great believer in a 'tangential' or 'oblique' marketing methods rather than direct approaches to achieve a marketing aim. These approaches work well in a consultancy market, which is a high value personal product. Direct approaches to sell must establish a client need, and information about the client, to discover whether a solution would be the right one. Bludgeoning the client to buy with a 'hard sell' from an uninformed position rarely produces results.

Exposure to clients and decision makers

Indirect marketing also works best by gaining access to the client for, say, a fact-finding opportunity, in an unthreatening, helpful way, looking for potential client solutions.

The potential client usually reacts well to this approach, and the consultant gains the benefit of inside knowledge of the client, and the opportunity to tailor a package of work to solve the client's problem. If it is established that the client needs different specialist help, that could also be an opportunity for any specialists in the network or elsewhere.

Bringing a clear solution to the client, even if it is not selling time directly this time round, puts a consultant in pole position for the next project, when and if it comes up.

'Trojan Horse' marketing

'Trojan Horse' marketing means utilising mechanisms to involve and engage potential clients using subtle indirect approaches, such as running surveys, writing a book, press and magazine articles, blogs or running seminars.

One tool that worked well for me in the consultancy business was running surveys on a variety of issues. The surveys had several areas of value:

- For clients as market intelligence
- For the respondents as positioning information
- For the publicity gained from publishing summaries of the results in newspapers and trade magazines
- Publishing the results

For a time, surveys became a big consultancy product for me, working with the marketing departments of several Banks. I produced market intelligence on the SME corporate banking market, and in one case, a survey developed into a sponsored published book (*The Chartered Institute of Bankers Directory of Corporate Banking, 1997)*.

Secret No. 37 Inventive indirect client approaches can be very productive

Next Action: Think about new approaches you could make where you can add value to your business proposition

How can a new business generate prospects?

There are many methods of prospect generation. It is worth trying different options to see what works best. Some methods are:

- Prospects from word of mouth and reputation
- Prospects from email marketing
- Prospects from electronic media – LinkedIn and Twitter
- Prospects from telephone marketing
- Prospects from mailshots
- Prospects via website or blog
- Prospects from publications, articles, newsletters and blogs.

Prospects from word of mouth and reputation

Repeat business, and prospects from the network, and old employers are the most valuable. This is the place to start, using a CRM system (as discussed before), to make sure that the balance of activity is enough to create interest and discussion, but not too much to be over-familiar or pushy.

Prospects from email marketing

This is cheap and easy to generate but wording of the message is vital. Using email with other techniques, such as:

- sending a reprint of a magazine article that is relevant or of interest
- drawing attention to a website may generate more traffic and possible leads.

Prospects from electronic media – LinkedIn and Twitter

Social media has changed how marketing works for new businesses, with networks such as LinkedIn offering a shop window and networking opportunities. Data is available for a fee showing who has interrogated the details, which could be valuable information.

Running a blog will provide statistics on pages viewed, which can be invaluable in helping to present the right image. Generating a strong following on Twitter could be very valuable, particularly in terms of creating the image of being an expert in a niche. The time spent needs to be balanced against the results achieved though. Beware networks of people selling and make sure your networks have buyers for your product or services.

Prospects from telephone marketing

Some small consultancies have traditionally used cold-calling telesales staff to generate appointments against a specific list of targets. A new business can do this themselves, if they are adept on the phone. This works better in some industries than others, but it may be worth trying.

Prospects from mailshots

With more and more marketing moving online, a hard copy letter can have impact, particularly if used with helpful topical information for the prospect. As discussed before, using cold mail shots, my success rate was low – the best achieved was 1% success rate for a client appointment.

Prospects via website or blog

A website should represent the business's stature and relevance properly. It should also generate leads and make it easy for people to get in touch. The new business can set out their stall in the website, and perhaps give away some freebies, such as articles and current useful information on their sector, expertise and knowledge to attract traffic.

I had a website that did not seek a large volume of hits, as I operated in a very specialist niche. I did, however, use the statistics generated from hits to look at how successful other forms of marketing were.

Customers will generally look at a website and do a Google search when carrying out due diligence about potential suppliers. It is worth prioritising search engine optimisation to ensure that typical Google search terms will bring your website to the top of the results.

Prospects from publications, articles, newsletters and blogs

For consultancy or professional businesses, writing articles and producing publications is an excellent way to raise a profile. It adds credibility and gravitas to a reputation. Businesses can also discover which channels might share content, or if influential bloggers in the field may be interested in guest posts. Shareable content will help develop a presence and keep traffic coming to the site. Paying for Google clicks in a specific situation may prove valuable.

Good marketing reduces the tension

Often, the main tension about being in business is covering the marketing properly and professionally while doing the work for the customer. This can be very challenging, requiring a high degree of multitasking ability as discussed before.

For solo consultants for example, going up a steep learning curve on a current project with the customer and being highly absorbed in delivery has a strong tendency to push any other activity including marketing into the background. Having a good marketing infrastructure and the discipline to have consistent levels of activity reduces this tension substantially.

Secret No. 38 Consistent and regular marketing activity reduces stress

Next Action: Make time for marketing activity, irrespective of how busy you are with delivery

Qualify leads carefully – especially from personal contacts

Once a business gets leads, looking at them with a very clear and open mind, and ranking them in order of real potential will be helpful.

The entrepreneur may want to be firm with those contacts or acquaintances that always want advice or product, but never seem to want to pay. There is a careful balance to be struck here about developing a relationship and demonstrating knowledge, and then monetising that relationship. Think carefully about your 'house rules' and how and where to draw the line.

Also beware of falling into the trap of chasing dreams without a very clear understanding of the risks. I was involved in several venture capital start-up projects with lots of potential work post-investment, as well as equity participation. They usually seemed to require a lot of up-front pro bono work. Projects like this broke my 'house rules', but an entrepreneur may feel that they need to follow some of them up, as I did. Do the sums carefully.

The acid test

The acid test I have used when approached by contacts with a proposition is simple:

are they selling?

Or:

are they buying?

If they are buying, that is usually a fantastic opportunity.

Secret No. 39 Beware contacts selling, not buying

Next Action: Review all prospects and close down those selling

Chapter 37 Negotiating the deals

You do not get what you want. You get what you negotiate.

Harvey Mackay – American Businessman

The basics of negotiation

Negotiation is a process by which people settle differences. It is a method by which compromise, or agreement is reached while avoiding argument and dispute.

In any disagreement, individuals understandably aim to achieve the best outcome for their position (or their organisation). However, the principles of fairness, seeking mutual benefit and maintaining a relationship are the keys to successful resolution that works for both parties.

We negotiate every day

We do everything in our daily lives by negotiating, from the mundane, such as which TV programme to watch, to buying a new car, or which supermarket to use.

From the major to the mundane, negotiating is the way we get things done. One of my clients told me 'my toughest negotiations are with my dog'.

Erica Ariel Fox – Harvard Law School.

What is valuable to the buyer in a negotiation?

Understanding what is valuable to the buyer is important. Different customers may have very different buying criteria. An accountant customer may solely buy on price, but a managing director customer may buy on criteria such as standing or reputation. The only way to establish the buyer's thinking is to ask the right questions, and to understand the customer. Understanding why the customer bought from you is a major impetus for future sales.

Entrepreneurs have to negotiate everything

Every successful negotiation is one more step on the journey to running a successful business, but not all entrepreneurs are natural or skilled negotiators. As negotiations take a large part in running any new business, it is worth having a view of your negotiating ability and strength. Take self-help or training steps to improve your negotiating skills if you think you need it, or even if you do not.

How good a negotiator are you?

You will need to be in a position that you can negotiate what you need, to be a business success.

Also, can you talk about prices and day rates without showing embarrassment? Are you tough enough, cool enough and logical enough to get what you need? Can you ask the right questions?

Establish a winning mindset and set goals you want to achieve. Imagine how it feels to win, and what is realistically achievable.

The start-up negotiating trap

Do not assume that you have a weak negotiating position just because you are starting in business. You have just as much right to negotiate a good deal as the next business. Also, your offering may bring new benefits that your customer has not had access to before, particularly if you are in a disruptive or new product market. The same principles apply to negotiating with external investors in your business.

Never assume that the balance of power is weighted against you, but look for your own strong negotiating angles, such as new product features, better service, or particular benefits.

Always look for a win-win deal

This is vital to understand. One side does not lose in a negotiation: both sides should win.

If you approach each deal on this basis, business can become more successful, and the good relationship generated with a customer or supplier can be very beneficial. Repeat business will also benefit both sides if they both win from each new transaction.

The process of negotiation

The simple outlines of the process of negotiation are:

- Preparation and planning – look at all the scenarios
- Think about the opening offer – it becomes the basis for all subsequent discussion, and is virtually impossible to change later
- Be unemotional and neutral
- Ask questions
- Understand your strengths and weaknesses
- Play the game – it is a game
- Develop an ability to think on your feet – you may have to improvise on the spot to keep a deal. This is where planning and preparation come into their own, as you will know your own 'red lines' which cannot be crossed
- Verbal ability is an important asset to engage constructively in bargaining

- Business, product or service knowledge adds depth to the offer
- Be helpful, but do not give too much information away for free
- Know when to walk away. This is a fundamental point, as some unscrupulous negotiators may push beyond fair limits
- Avoid a bad deal
- Close the deal positively and take away written confirmation

Everything is negotiable all the time

Think about the duration and terms of each deal, and remember that as circumstances change, often deals may be subject to renegotiation.

Secret No. 40 Learn to negotiate the best deals you need to run the business well

Next Action: Be very well prepared for every negotiation

Chapter 38 Back office: Scorekeeping and administration

The 18,000 NASA employees are full of galactic talents and abilities and are ready to accomplish whatever they're directed to do.

P. J. O'Rourke – US Journalist

Keeping score well helps you win

Doing the administration, and keeping score can often be drudgery, and the unexciting part of the operation.

There may be a temptation to do the exciting, order-winning parts of the business, and leave the administrative tasks until, perhaps, the end of the month or the weekends. Depending on their different backgrounds, some entrepreneurs will have greater experience than others in dealing with administration. Fortunately, modern technology helps provide solutions.

The aim is to develop a 'feel' and understanding

As you run a new business, you will develop a 'feel' and understanding for the numbers and information about your business. This knowledge gets deeper with time and will help enormously in making the right judgement calls. There will be difficult decisions and negotiations coming down the track.

Data vs. information

What is the difference? Data are raw unorganised facts that require some processing to be put in useful form. When data is properly organised, analysed and presented, it becomes information, which is usable and understandable.

Good information (management information) is what drives a business.

A monthly sales shortfall

A simple example would be knowing the sales value of one invoice (say, £120 out of many sales transactions), against the monthly total sales value (say, £10,000).

The £10,000 total figure is valuable information, particularly if the monthly sales target is £11,000. The shortfall of monthly sales of £1,000 is good management information that can be acted on, to make sure that the target will be met next month. The individual sales value of £120 is just data.

If you don't measure it, you can't control it!

A new business will generate lots of data, especially at transactional levels (like the £120 sales invoice).

Having good information enables business owners to keep score, because if the business has good information, it can manage the day-to-day changes needed, to be able to survive and prosper.

Mobile and PC systems give information

In the past, all this data was analysed by hand to produce good information by teams of clerks. Fortunately, now mobile and PC systems generally provide very good information for running a business and can cover most of the back office functions needed for effective management.

Back office functions – an overview

This is an overview of back office functions generally needed (not an exhaustive list):

- Accounting – invoicing, receivables, payables, general ledger, cashbook, VAT, PAYE, other taxes
- Management information needed to run the business
- HR and employees, payroll, pensions
- Legal, company secretarial, corporate governance, board meetings and minutes (for a limited company)

'Keep It Simple, Stupid' (KISS), automated and on your mobile phone or tablet

I spent a lifetime in accounting, requiring massive systems supported by many people to provide good management information. Small businesses were not well catered for, and accounting and information systems were almost an end in themselves.

Now, the modern world is very different because there are many good tools to make the back office simple and effective.

Information available electronically can be tailored to an entrepreneur's needs with no army of clerical support staff and is potentially available in the palm of the hand.

KISS – use mobile tools wherever possible.

What things are important to measure?

Every business will have different information requirements, but the following is a list of some items that

I have found useful to measure, by category and against a budget. You can pick and mix for your particular business.

Marketing

- Marketing activity by channel
- Total leads
- Total qualified leads
- Lead conversion rate
- Order bank
- Order pipeline

Production and Stock

- Monthly production units
- Stock by units and value
- Stock turn (how often the stock turns over per year)

Sales

- Sales by product unit and value
- Gross margin by product and value

Overheads

- Costs by type against budget

Receivables (money due in)

- Total receivables value
- Aged receivables (30, 60, 90, 120 days)
- Average age of receivables

Payables (money due out)

- Total payables value
- Aged payables (30, 60, 90, 120 days)
- Average age of payables

Cash

- Daily and monthly cash balance

- Budget cash inflows and outflows

Some ideas to speed things up

- **Invoice electronically** – use software to email your invoice when the job is finished and delivered. Do not wait to invoice until the end of the week or month – it will affect your cashflow
- **Collect payments electronically**, ideally when you have invoiced, by card if possible. There is more detail about this in Chapter 39
- **Use a simple spreadsheet (Excel or Numbers**) coupled with electronic banking and mobile accounting software on a tablet or phone, so you are always up to date

Scorekeeping – a case study in hairdressing

As part of my Prince's Trust mentoring, I helped Kelly set up a new hairdressing salon. After the salon had been up and running for a few weeks, we talked about the need to understand the numbers, such as how many customers per day there were, sales per day, costs and so on.

Kelly said: 'I can't do that – I'm crap at maths, my schoolteacher told me I was.'

'This is not maths, it's hairdressing – how happy are you using Excel?'

'I can use Excel, no problem.'

We agreed a list of data to collect, and the next month Kelly had a complete set of graphs, and good management information about her business, including how school holidays affected her turnover, and when to anticipate lulls in business. She invested in another barber's chair and brought in a part-time hairdresser to expand the business.

Kelly was on it, and had great control of her back office, and she successfully later sold the business, having built it up from scratch.

Secret No. 41 Have at your fingertips, the right mobile systems that you need to run the business

Next Action: Get comfortable with, and know your business numbers inside out

Part 7 – Cash and costs

Chapter 39 Cash is king

Revenue is vanity, profit is sanity, but cash is king.

Anonymous

Never take your eyes off the cash flow, because it's the lifeblood of the business.

Richard Branson – British business magnate

The importance of cash flow

Cash flow is what makes or breaks a new business, or any business, so this is one of the most important chapters in this book.

Cash flow is a minefield, particularly for new businesses starting out. Without the right knowledge and planning for how their cash flow will work, there are many traps for the unwary. Here are some of the basics:

Trade credit

Trade credit allows businesses to receive goods or services in exchange for a promise to pay the supplier within a set amount of time, normally 30, 60, 90 or 120 days as part of the supply contract. The supplier will send an invoice showing the amount payable, VAT if applicable, and terms of payment.

The creditors ledger or payables section in the customers' accounts department will process the invoice on their books and then generally ignore the terms of payment.

The customer usually pays the bill when it suits them, unless special arrangements have been made. More on this later.

Eventually the bill will be paid, sometimes as late as 90 to 120 days or more. The spectrum of payment can be as little as 5 to 7 days to more than 120 days.

Can trade credit work to your advantage?

Ice cream scenario A

If, for example, a business can buy products on, say, 60-day terms and sell it for cash (such as ice cream), the business will have positive cash flow from day 1.

Widgets scenario B

The reverse is also true – if a business pays cash for widgets, and then gives 60 days' credit on the sale, the business must finance each sale for 60 days, which will be a substantial burden, and will need borrowing or capital to cover it.

Self-funding ice cream or more borrowings for widgets

In Scenario A, growing the ice cream business will be self-financing – it is just a case a selling more ice cream for cash.

Growing the widget business will be tough, because every new contract will require financing for 60 days, so borrowings will increase. The widget supplier has to be in two businesses – widgets and finance.

Trade credit is a huge source of funding

There is a long history of abuse by wealthy customers taking too long to pay their bills, starting in the 17th and 18th century with the aristocracy. This abuse continues to the present day.

Typically, in the 18th century, an aristocratic household could take a year or more to pay local suppliers for food and drink or building maintenance work.

Despite much lobbying by small and medium companies, many large companies have taken the historical place of the aristocracy in the current economy as bad payers.

Managing supplier payments

Existing companies protect their cash flow by paying out the minimum to their suppliers, while paying their salaries and other costs. Trade credit, as we have seen, is a major form of finance for some businesses.

For example, Walmart, the largest retailer in the world, based in the USA, has used trade credit from its suppliers as a larger source of capital than bank borrowings. Trade credit for Walmart is eight times the capital invested by shareholders (*Wikipedia*). This is the ice cream model of business (Scenario A) mentioned earlier.

Walmart suppliers have to be in two businesses: providing both products and banking facilities to their customer

Walmart's suppliers act as its bankers. Why should they do this?

One of Walmart's top sellers is paper towels. The towel manufacturer will have done their sums carefully to meet Walmart's requirements for a very competitive price, and a large volume of orders, but also will factor in how long

Walmart take to pay. The payment terms from Walmart will be on a 'take it or leave it' basis.

The towel manufacturer now has two businesses – making paper products, and also banking. They also have a cash flow problem, because they will need to invest substantially to upgrade capacity to handle the volume of Walmart's business.

Fortunately, in the USA a financing industry has grown up around Walmart especially for suppliers with this problem. Those solutions, however, come at a cost, are complex, and take time to set up. The cost must be factored into the Walmart price for paper towels.

Trade credit is a huge source of business problems for small businesses

In the early stages of setting up a new business, it is very easy for the business to fall into the trap of giving too much credit to customers. Those new customers will gladly take credit from a new, inexperienced supplier. Those customers also may not be a good credit risk and may not pay their bills.

Don't fall into the trade credit trap – giving too much credit to win business, without having the right financing in place. Always make sure your customers can pay.

How trade credit works in practice – the financial director's tale

In the days when there were cheques, as a company finance director (FD), I would decide on a Thursday which suppliers could be paid from a list by cheque on the Friday for that week.

I could only pay out a fixed amount, as pressing items needed to be paid, such as salaries or PAYE, which have to be paid on fixed dates.

Every Friday, I signed a mountain of cheques. The payments may be electronic now, but the process is much the same (one signature instead of hundreds).

There were always 'urgent' payments at the top of the list that had to be made to maintain supply, avoid legal action, or to take discounts. The suppliers who chased their debt badly would have to wait…….a long time.

FDs today work the same way and will only usually pay early if there are special arrangements, or discounts.

Fight to get prompt payment

As a consultant, I always ensured that my invoices were contractually payable in seven days, and that the FD or managing director (MD) signed my contract.

You can guess what happened when I started work with the new client, and the first invoice was due. I phoned credit control and they would always say that the invoice would be paid in 60 days on standard terms.

I pointed out that this breached my contract, signed by the FD (or MD), and that they would want to pay it on time.

It always took a few weeks for the credit control department to learn to pay my invoice promptly, which they all invariably did in the end.

It takes consistency and persistence, and a good (normally contractual) case to be paid sooner than normal terms.

Secret No. 42 Your customers will love you lending them your money for 90 days if you let them

Next Action: Find a way on payments to be a 'special case' and be paid early, or end up waiting like the rest of the herd

So, what should new businesses do?

Does your business need to give trade credit? For example, Chris the Plumber (who we met earlier) takes deposits from customers by credit or debit card, and then agreed stage payments, also by card. On completion of the work, final payment will be taken using a debit or credit card for the electronic invoice while at the customers' premises, having signed off the work.

Many tradespeople might be embarrassed to ask for money at the end of the job, or not be organised enough to have an invoice already prepared. They also may not have the equipment needed to process card payments on their phones when the job is complete.

They will become unwitting bankers to their customers for however long the customer takes to pay.

New disruptive businesses need not follow the credit 'rules' or play 'the game' to the same extent

Internet-based businesses, particularly 'disruptors' (which we saw in Chapter 15) usually have the intrinsic benefit of being outside the normal payment terms or cycle for their customers. They can often ask for cash up-front or on delivery by credit card, while taking credit where possible from their suppliers. This often puts them into the 'ice cream' category of generating cash while taking credit from suppliers.

For those that have to play the 'credit game'

Giving trade credit is a last resort, so if you have no choice but to give trade credit as part of your business, it is important to tightly control what you give, and to whom:

- Get credit ratings for all your customers, through such sources as Dunn & Bradstreet or Experian
- Review the ratings and put credit limits on accounts if needed
- Refuse credit to poorly rated customers – insist on cash up-front
- Think about different pricing for differently credit rated customers
- Offer cash discounts for immediate settlement (making sure the funds clear before you deliver)
- Chase your debt unmercifully **all the time** – this will take time and cost money. Think about it as a 'training scheme' for your customers. You want them to think (especially the FD) that if your business is not in the payment run this week, that they will be hassled unmercifully until the bill is paid, or supplies will dry up
- Look at raising funding from factoring (borrowings based on outstanding invoices) or other sources for your debts if your business is right for it, and you can recover the costs

You may think this is too much hassle or costs too much.

Think again – the first bad debt you have will usually cost several times more than the administrative cost of getting that customer to pay you on time in the first place. Your business survival, profitability and cash flow depends on a consistent, powerful and professional approach.

Secret No. 43 Chase your debtors unmercifully all the time

Next Action: Look to speed up cashflow with discounts or promotions. Be tough on customers that are bad payers

Problems with payments

Be well prepared – have the information you need to hand to chase for the money that customers owe you.

Even if you chase customers unmercifully for your cash, you are likely to have late payments or bad debts if you give credit.

Only deal with customers that are good payers

This is a tough issue. Business instinct is to take on all business irrespective. In choosing not to take some business, you may lose a certain volume of trade, but the cash flow will be better for it, and generally the entrepreneur (in my experience) can sleep better at night.

Late payment and bad debts

Develop a clear policy of what to do and when, for escalating action for late payment. This section does not provide a detailed plan on credit control, as that information is available elsewhere. The idea here is to provide some pointers and strategies that can work. The secret is consistency and regularity, so that the customer is 'trained' into taking the right action.

A suggested debt collection process based on 30 days credit given

Stage	Action
Order	Credit check the customer Decline business if poor Look at cash or stage payments to reduce risk
Delivery or performance of service	Invoice as quickly as possible
Invoice	Ensure invoice and delivery received by customer – not 'lost in the post'
20 days	Send statement and due date reminder
30 Days	Receive payment. If not chase, with statement and reminder
45 Days	Stop new supply or services if appropriate
60 Days	Take legal or collection action

You can take legal action yourself

Taking legal action – you can use the Small Claims Court for debts up to £10,000, with a scale of fees applicable up to 4.5% of the value. I have used this system myself to good effect. Other remedies are available, such as using debt recovery agents, or issuing a Winding Up Petition.

These can be potentially more complex and expensive solutions.

Secret No. 44 If you give credit, try to sell only to solvent customers that you have checked out

Next Action: Run credit checks on all new customers and offer the right terms for a good credit rating. Cash in advance for poor quality customers allows you to sleep better at night

What happens if a customer goes bust?

If you did deal with that bad customer, and they went bust what happens, and will you get your money back?

Normally, a debt to another business becomes an unsecured creditor in a winding up or liquidation. This means that when the administrator collects all the money the bust business has, it will pay out on secured debts first, such as bank loans or mortgages. Unsecured creditors (the debt) are way down the pecking order, and as result only normally get a few pence in the pound of their debt, if anything at all is left.

Chapter 40 Keeping costs down

He helped us through financial crisis after crisis and was willing to take the tough decisions to reduce costs on the many occasions that we had overstretched ourselves. Famously – to make a point – even rationing tea, biscuits and lavatory paper!

Richard Branson on Nik Powell (1950–2019) – his childhood friend and original partner in Virgin Records

Richard Branson and Nik Powell

Richard Branson started Virgin Records with his childhood friend, Nik Powell. Nik was Richard Branson's 'numbers and money man' who 'kept the show on the road'. The Virgin 'show' went quite a way down the road.

Nik was also exceptionally good at negotiating deals and paying absolutely no more than was necessary for any business expense.

Nik parted company with Richard Branson, and had a successful career working in the film industry. I was lucky enough to work for Nik for seven months as his FD a few years ago.

Nik, unfortunately, is no longer with us, but he has since become a model for me on how to approach costs and overheads when running a business.

Everything is negotiable – only accept the lowest cost

For Nik, everything was negotiable, and he would only accept the lowest possible cost base he could, while maintaining quality. He was invariably very clever and thoughtful about ways of reducing or minimising costs.

He was also very stubborn about getting to the cost level he had set in his mind. This generated a lot of hassle, but the results on the bottom line were always very positive.

Get Nik's mindset or find someone who has it

As the story shows, there are great benefits in sharing responsibilities when growing a business or controlling cash and costs through difficult times. An entrepreneur has to do both the growing and controlling, so if they can only build the business, they clearly should seek help, or find a partner that can.

Secret No. 45 Use Nik Powell's mindset: be inventive and ruthless on negotiating and reducing costs

Next Action: Think about clever ways you can set up the business with the lowest possible cost base. Always push the envelope to reduce costs

Part 8 – Survival and growth

Chapter 41 Support groups

There is no such thing as a self-made man. You will reach your goals only with the help of others.

George Shinn – US Sports Business Owner

Everybody needs help and support

As we have seen in the previous chapter, Richard Branson had help from Nik Powell on his way to great success. Help and support can come in many forms, and from different groups.

The importance of partners and a support infrastructure

Support from a partner, if the entrepreneur has one, is fundamental to success. If the partner can bring some expertise or experience to help, it will make a substantial difference to the level of success. This support particularly applies to strategy.

Any management consultant knows that nearly all their clients have difficulty seeing their own businesses with clarity and perspective (the 'wood from the trees' – this is one of the reasons that management consultancy thrives).

The same rules apply to a new business. It is likely that an entrepreneur's shortcomings and areas for review will remain stubbornly invisible to them, and they will need help.

Having an independent sounding board, a critical friend, or a partner who can give an independent view, is very important in those long-term strategic plans and critical decisions. If the partner fulfils that role, and can add value to the business, it is very fortunate.

Using social media and online forums such as Facebook and LinkedIn can help in 'joining up' a lot of individual thinking, and create a virtual network, which can be both helpful and supportive.

Secret No. 46 Entrepreneurs benefit by sharing and developing their knowledge within networks to make up for their lack of infrastructure and support

Next Action: Use a partner, friend or previous colleague as a sounding board

Chapter 42 What could possibly go wrong?

It took us a couple seconds to really realise that we had made it. And then the people in the viewing room start stomping, and I mean just cheering and clapping and stomping their feet. I'm so tied up emotionally at this time that I literally cannot speak, and I've got to get my team back on track.

[It took a physical act to get him back to reality].

I rapped my arm on the console — and break my pencil! — and finally get back on track and call my controllers to attention. I say, 'OK, all you flight controllers, settle down. OK. Let's get back on with it.'

Gene Kranz –NASA Flight Director, on the successful Apollo 11 Moon landing after major challenges including radio problems, a computer malfunction and low fuel nearly forcing an abort for the whole Moon mission at touchdown on the Moon.

Apollo 11 only just made it to the Moon

On the Apollo 11 flight, nearly everything went wrong all at once at the most critical stage in the mission. The tremendous team dealt with the issues and solved the problems by literally 'flying by the seat of their pants' and falling back on their great training and preparation.

As with Moon missions, life and business are risky, with traps for the unwary.

Take positive action in troubling times

This chapter is about remaining positive during the problems that arise ('the glass half full'), while fully planning and anticipating the issues that will come from being negative ('the glass half empty').

Remain positive, while considering what is likely to happen. Over-optimism is potentially deadly.

If it can go wrong, it probably will

The first thing to consider is to have a backup plan for worst case scenarios that may arise. This does not necessarily have to be detailed, but a clear strategy and mindset that can be switched on as a 'battle plan' when times get tough.

I was involved in several company rescues, and often fell back on a 'war room' approach – the whole executive team meeting on a regular daily basis to consider plans, and implement new approaches to tight deadlines, often the next day. There is more on this approach in Chapter 48.

Be conservative in the good times

The second thing to consider is that 'repairing the roof while the sun shines' is one of those sayings that really works.

Be very conservative in the good times. Stash the cash and be strong when competitors are potentially weak and 'splashing the cash'.

Money in the bank in a time of crisis is more valuable than gold.

It's not easy, be prepared, be resilient

At the time of writing the Coronavirus (COVID-19) is seriously affecting many businesses, the economy and government.

It is early days yet, but many businesses are likely to have deadly wounds, such as the impacts on the hospitality, airline and travel businesses, while others must contend with a boom at a time of short supply. These include supermarkets, medical companies and makers of cleaning products.

Some large businesses may be regretting paying large dividends to shareholders, instead of building up a 'rainy day' fund that can take advantage of opportunities when times are tough: EasyJet, for example have paid out over £1bn in dividends over recent years. Imagine their strength now had they retained the cash, and the potential to consolidate their competition and market.

Secret No. 47 Everything can go wrong at any time, but if it does, it always means the cash flow is under pressure

Next Action: Keep a 'rainy day' cash reserve if you can in the business and have a simple disaster plan. Use the 'war room' approach if required

Chapter 43 Lessons from the greatest entrepreneur ever?

All the adversity I've had in my life, all my troubles and obstacles, have strengthened me... You may not realise it when it happens, but a kick in the teeth may be the best thing in the world for you.

Walt Disney

Over the years, there have been many great entrepreneurs operating in many fields, such as Henry Ford, Andrew Carnegie, Thomas Edison, Bill Gates, Oprah Winfrey Larry Page, Lakshmi Mittal, Richard Branson, and Steve Jobs amongst others.

Walter Elias Disney

For me, one of the greatest entrepreneurs was Walt Disney (Walter Elias Disney 1901–1966).

His story is amazing, and his legacy is huge:

- Cartoon characters like Mickey Mouse and Donald Duck
- Pioneering use of new technology – talkies and cartoons
- Pioneering feature length cartoons (*Snow White and the Seven Dwarfs*), and pushing the boundaries with art and music (*Fantasia*) and many songs that became standards
- Amusement parks: Disneyland in California and Walt Disney World in Florida and Paris
- The Disney Company – films and entertainment

What makes the story so valuable is the unshakeable vision he had, while overcoming the most difficult of times. The adversity he overcame, including being bankrupt several times, to be successful, is astonishing.

Early career

Brought up in the Mid-West, Disney was interested in art and graphic design. He wanted to be a newspaper cartoonist. In World War I he was an ambulance driver for the Red Cross in France and Germany.

Disney met a talented artist, Ub Iwerks, and in 1920 after their first business start-up 'Laugh-O-Gram' failed, they filed for bankruptcy **(the first time)**.

They worked together for a company in Kansas City producing animated advertisements for cinemas. Iwerks was a fast and flexible artist, and Disney was a creative visionary with a talent for selling.

In 1923 Disney set up his second business, making advertising films and cartoons. A New York firm cheated them, and they were forced to file for bankruptcy in 1923 (**the second time**).

Disney drove to California to be near the new film industry, and with his brother Roy set up his third business. This produced Mickey Mouse in 1928 and many other cartoons.

Disney survived the Great Depression of the 1930s, but nearly went bankrupt again in 1937 (**nearly the third time**) owing to mounting costs completing the feature film *Snow White and the Seven Dwarfs.*

The rest, as they say, is history.

Secret No. 48 There will be bumps in the road and major challenges for any business

Next Action: Consider how resilient Walt Disney was to come back from bankruptcy and major adversity several times in order to achieve his dream

Chapter 44 Staying in business: important things to remember

I'm convinced that about half of what separates successful entrepreneurs from the non-successful ones is pure perseverance.

Steve Jobs – founder of Apple

A never-ending series of challenges

Business is a never-ending challenge. That is what makes running a business so interesting and rewarding.

Perseverance is what makes the difference, and also being prepared to go the extra mile to keep on track.

Staying on track means having the answers to key questions that will keep on cropping up, sometimes at the worst possible moment.

Stay on track by knowing 'where you are'

Going forward, the answers to ten questions can generally tell whether a business is in the right shape or not:

Stay in business using 'the ten key things to manage day-to-day':

1. Do I have enough cash to pay the salaries this month (and the PAYE and the VAT if applicable)?
2. Is there enough work for next month in my marketing funnel (and the three months after that)?
3. If there is not enough work, what can I do urgently to rectify the position?

4. Can I deliver all the work I have on time and at the right cost?
5. Is my pricing correct and will I make a profit on my current level of business?
6. Am I up to speed on my competitors' activities?
7. Can I look back in detail over the history of my business in my management reports?
8. What future developments are going to affect my market?
9. Am I totally up to date with tax, Companies House filings and administrative tasks?
10. What do I need to do differently today to have a more successful and better business tomorrow?

Good luck on the journey and enjoy it!

Secret No. 49 Stay on track by answering 'The ten key things to manage day-to-day'

Next Action: What can I do differently to have a more successful and better business?

Part 9 – Coronavirus COVID-19 and their impacts

Chapter 45 Coronavirus: what has happened?

Would you like to know how it feels to be in the hospitality business during the Coronavirus pandemic?

Remember when the Titanic was sinking, and the band continued to play? Well, we're the band….

Anonymous

Resetting to the new normal is hard.

McKinsey & Co. – Global Management Consultants

Lockdown

At the time of writing, the UK is in major lockdown because of the Coronavirus pandemic. Businesses and the self-employed are being bailed out by government, while many employees are being laid off or furloughed.

Even though the Government has temporarily relaxed the laws around insolvent trading, many businesses will find it difficult to survive. We look to be at the beginning of what could be a long haul, where the fallout and economic impact could inevitably be substantial, with perhaps 30% of UK economic output (GDP, or Gross Domestic Product) temporarily lost.

A tectonic plate shift to a 'new normal'

Business-wise, we are now in uncharted territory. A once-in-a-century tectonic plate shift has occurred, and the results are difficult to foresee. We do know that it will differ greatly from what has gone before.

A crystal ball

Writing this part of the book requires a crystal ball, and they are not known for their forecasting accuracy. This section outlines my current view of what may happen in the Coronavirus crisis, but it needs to be heavily qualified.

Events may turn out differently, depending on the time taken to develop vaccines, and to run antibody and infection tests on the population. It also depends on how many businesses survive intact, and how well and quickly the banks and Government bail them out.

Hindsight

Hindsight will be a wonderful thing when it becomes available. We think at the moment it may take over six months to get back to some kind of normality, but nobody knows for sure at the time of writing.

Chapter 46 Coronavirus: consequences and risks

Events, dear boy, events

Attributed to British prime minister, Harold Macmillan, when asked by a journalist what was most likely to blow governments off course.

It's all up in the air and will come down differently

Major business opportunities could arise from these changes. When things change after major worldwide events (e.g. Spanish Flu, World War I, World War II), they often change irrevocably and there is no going back.

There will be a few winners from Coronavirus in businesses such as in healthcare, the internet, and some food and drink companies.

There will, however, be many more losers, across a huge range of industries. Many businesses will fail through no fault of their own, as they have been forced to shut their doors for so long. Some will fail because they have been weakened by poor management or greedy shareholders. Lack of cash will be the universal factor.

'Zombie' businesses will fail

A zombie company is a company that needs bailouts in order to operate, or an indebted company that is able to repay the interest on its debts but not repay the principal.

Wikipedia

An analysis by international accountants KPMG in May 2019 showed that one in seven UK firms could be categorised as 'zombie' companies, meaning that a small adverse change in economic circumstances would be fatal for them.

It is likely these companies will be some of the first to hit the wall. These under-resourced, under-capitalised and over-borrowed 'zombie' businesses could have a major problem with a two-week cash flow problem. A six months cash flow crisis is untenable.

Many good businesses will fail as well

The irony is that many good, well run businesses are also likely to fail alongside the poor ones. The virus does not discriminate in its human or its economic victims.

A major impact on business start-ups

As if setting up a new business were not challenging enough in normal times, now a new layer of complexity and challenge has been added with the Coronavirus. It will change new business start-ups substantially.

In compensation, in times of crisis many opportunities open up that would have seemed impossible in normal circumstances and times.

A shortage of funding

The main impact I can see is the impact on cash and funding for start-ups.

What, if any, funding will be available for start-ups? Huge amounts of government and bank lending will have gone into the bail-out of existing businesses, the self-employed and the furloughing of existing employees.

Will the banks lend?

Major banks might be weakened, having gone through the difficulties of the credit crunch. They also have managements and shareholders with lifestyles they have not, so far, been prepared to change. They traditionally have a history of never lending enough to SMEs, which I previously surveyed and wrote about.

There are also further credit problems on the way, such as the large 'bubble' in car finance, personal credit card debt, and loan syndication. Let us be honest, banks do not have a good track record of supporting businesses in difficult times. It remains to be seen if they will now 'step up to the plate'.

Government support

The Government has several programmes to stimulate current business and start-ups through grants and loans. These are well worth exploring for new businesses, but as they are subject to change, it is best to consult the advice on the Government website. Follow the research guidelines outlined in Chapter 16. Ensure that time spent on looking for funding is wisely spent, and that not too much time is wasted.

Chapter 47 Coronavirus: opportunities and rewards

There may be a shift from just-in-time to just in case.
Mark Cliffe – ING Bank

What is the status quo?

Any business today that embraces the status quo as an operating principle is going to be on a death march.
Howard Schultz – CEO Starbucks

The status quo is defined as *the present situation or condition.*

At the time of writing, we have seen that the status quo has just changed substantially and suddenly (see Chapter 46)

Many businesses and the operation of government are predicated on stable circumstances and ordered markets, and the smooth operation of the status quo. This has now all changed.

Unfortunately, as we have seen, many businesses (both good and bad) might fail during or after the Coronavirus lockdown. They cannot deal with the rapid change in circumstances, or the lack of cash in the economy.

Major events

Major events, such as Coronavirus, challenge businesses, politicians and government. Businesses that are both nimble and flexible will have the potential to ride out the challenges that will inevitably arise.

Governments and institutions are, by their nature, inflexible. They are driven by policy, which takes time to agree and change. They can therefore usually only demonstrate flexibility in times, such as now, of national emergency

The mould is broken – it will be different

Attitudes and methods are only changed in a major crisis, otherwise the status quo persists with only minor tinkering round the edges. There are examples below.

There will be shortages of some products, and major opportunities

The supply chain from the Far East was well run, and virtually invisible to retail customers here in Europe.

The products you buy here in the UK, electrical or electronic goods (such as an iron, a kettle or a phone), are on the shelf and the prices are very good value. The choice is bewildering.

Those products take many weeks to get here, and there was a continuous conveyor belt of ships carrying containers from Far East factories to constantly top up demand here in Europe. Stocks will have been optimised to a minimum in the supply chain to match demand on a seasonal basis.

Deliveries from the Far East: some rough estimates on timing:

Order lead time, say	4 weeks
Manufacturing lead time, say	4 weeks
Shipping time by sea, say	8 weeks

So, in normal times the lead time is, say, around 16 weeks, or four months.

Opportunities to fill the vacuum

The inescapable position remains that the UK market could be short of an available volume of consumer and other products for anything up to a year, with demand coming back slowly from virtually zero in lockdown in the UK.

There may be a large vacuum to fill with local, quality products, that are immediately available.

Clean up time for businesses with cash

Those businesses with cash, including those recently successful hedge funds and venture capitalists, will be seeking to buy existing good, but cash-strapped, businesses for knock-down prices.

Those very conservative businesses that have held on to their positive cash flow also now have a major opportunity to buy out their competitors for knock-down prices and clean up.

Herein lies the opportunity

A major window of opportunity has opened for new and existing strong businesses. Those new businesses, who can take over, and use different approaches will provide foundations for the future.

The time for innovation is now: nimble and flexible will win

Now is the time to innovate and push forward with new ideas. Many new industries might emerge with opportunities that Coronavirus has created. There will also be different products and services using novel approaches or delivery channels to replace old businesses as they fall by the wayside.

Some businesses may build on recent technology which has not yet become mainstream. For example, with the onset of Coronavirus we have seen the rise in contactless payments, and the decline of cash. Using existing companies such as PayPal could fuel the next generation of innovation. Building a flexible and nimble way of thinking into your planning will help win in these new times.

Hedge your bets

Try not to rely on single markets, single methods of distribution, large customers or a few products.

Spread or hedge your bets to leave options open if circumstances change. The examples below show that narrow approaches without alternatives can, in the post-Coronavirus world be damaging or catastrophic.

Milk down the drain

At a local level, during the Coronavirus lockdown I read about a dairy farmer throwing away 6,000 litres of milk every day. He had no means of packaging his milk for the retail market in lockdown. He had specialised in providing milk in bulk containers specifically for coffee shops. The market he relied on had literally dried up, and the farmer had no alternative means of packaging and distributing his products, even though he could have sold all his output.

The tale of two greengrocers

Locally, we have two greengrocers we used regularly to buy fruit and vegetables in normal times. Their retail markets disappeared overnight with the lockdown, but high demand remained for their products.

Greengrocer A converted quickly to an online platform with collections and local deliveries during the lockdown.

Greengrocer B tried but failed to convert from a normal retail environment to an online store. The learning curve and the time pressure must have been too much.

Being both nimble, flexible and having the capability to change markets and types of distribution can be the difference between survival and failure in challenging market circumstances.

Resilience

The new watchword for businesses will be resilience. Building resilience into any business after Coronavirus will be essential. Managing customers in a flexible way and adapting to changes in circumstances quickly will help extend survivability.

Likely survival scenarios

Many businesses could fail through the crisis with strong businesses likely to be weakened, and weak businesses not surviving at all.

Businesses – possible impact of Coronavirus

Relative strength pre-Coronavirus	**Post-Coronavirus**
Strong	OK
OK	Weak
Weak	Dead

Ian Mackey BBF

Heightened awareness to developments and risks

What else might happen in this new world? There will be a heightened awareness, almost paranoia, about what could happen to affect businesses. The 'threats' part of the SWOT analysis will need to be revisited, and also perhaps a new lease of life given to risk registers.

New emphasis on risk registers

A risk register is a tool for documenting risks, and actions to manage each risk. The risk register is essential to the successful management of risk. As risks are identified they are logged on the register and actions are taken to respond to the risk.

stakeholdermap.com

Risk registers have traditionally been part of the business planning process, and one of those bureaucratic exercises that used to be repeated every year, in order to tick the appropriate box.

No longer – the story goes that in 2019, at the top of the Government risk register was the threat of a new pandemic.

Chapter 48 Coronavirus: a winning mindset

Setting up a new business just got a lot tougher

The ultimate measure of a man is not where he stands in moments of comfort and convenience, but where he stands at times of challenge and controversy.

Martin Luther King, Jr. –American Christian minister and activist (applies to all genders)

Overcoming the fear: the power of mindset

The new post-Coronavirus business world is, and will be, scary. Learning to develop mindsets that can cope with the pressures and challenges in the new world that will emerge are fundamental. We have seen in Chapter 8 that entrepreneurs need special characteristics, and that in Chapter 43, a strong mindset can achieve anything in very adverse circumstances.

General Montgomery's plan for D-Day

I worked in South London for a client for a few months several years ago and was lucky to be able to visit the Imperial War Museum over lunch times, as it was within easy walking distance of my office.

In 1945, two months before D-Day, General Montgomery sketched out in pencil on one piece of paper, his vision for the invasion of Europe. The invasion used hundreds of ships and aircraft, and 140,000 troops. As we all know, it was a successful operation that changed the progress of the War.

I saw this old piece of brown paper in the Museum, covered in pencil notes. It looked like it had been written on the back of an envelope. I was astonished that the original idea for the whole D-Day operation was outlined on this one page. I loved the notes, with '*the key note of everything to be 'SIMPLICITY'*', triple underlined:

General Montgomery's One Page D-Day Plan

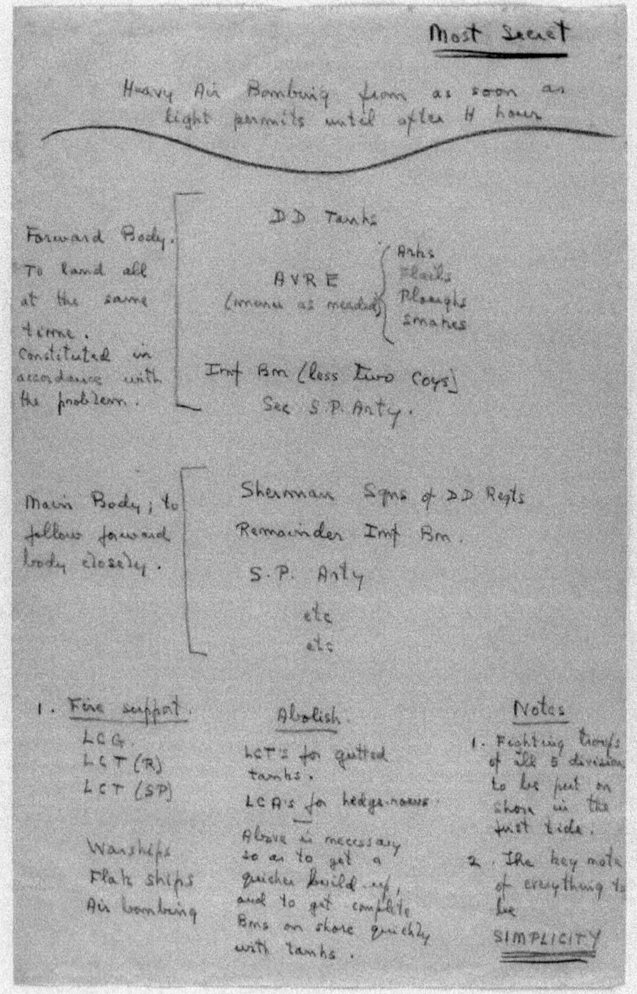

Most Secret

Heavy Air Bombing from as soon as light permits until after H hour

Forward Body. To land all at the same time. Constituted in accordance with the problem.

- D.D. Tanks
- AVRE (menu as needed): Arks, Flails, Ploughs, Snakes
- Inf Bn (less two Coys)
- Sec S.P. Arty.

Main Body; to follow forward body closely.

- Sherman Sqns of DD Regts
- Remainder Inf Bn.
- S.P. Arty
- etc
- etc

1. Fire support.
LCG.
LCT (R)
LCT (SP)

Warships
Flak ships
Air bombing

Abolish.
LCT's for gutted tanks.
LCA's for hedge-hogs.
Above is necessary so as to get a quicker build-up, and to get complete Bns on shore quickly with tanks.

Notes
1. Fighting troops of all 5 divisions to be put on shore in the first tide.
2. The key note of everything to be SIMPLICITY

© Imperial War Museum (Documents.20501/D)

The Montgomery mindset

Imagine the mindset Montgomery had, when thinking about this plan. Britain was suffering bombings, and was on the back foot, and the D-Day Plan must have been considered 'do or die' for the country. He got on with the job, and the rest is history.

The best plans have modest beginnings

Some of the best plans have been put onto one piece of paper and shown that the worst of circumstances can be overcome.

Chapter 49 Coronavirus: major long-term changes

If you want to lose 40 pounds, you order salad instead of fries. If you want to be a better friend, you take the phone call instead of screening it. If you want to write a novel, you sit down and write a single paragraph. It's scary to make major changes, but we usually have enough courage to take the next right step.

Regina Brett – Author

The next right step

The Coronavirus pandemic is not an excuse for entrepreneurs to do nothing, or to wait until the situation improves. As the quotation suggests, make a small start, but make a start.

Some changes will be forced by circumstance and necessity, and there will be a sea change in corporate attitudes. These changes become opportunities for new businesses to exploit.

Next steps in corporate attitudes

A wide range of corporate attitudes might change such as:

- Working from home
- How capitalism works
- Ecology and the environment
- A kinder, more caring society

Here is one example of major change that came from a natural catastrophe. In August 2017, Hurricane Harvey hit Houston, Texas with massive impact. BP's office was flooded, and needed the removal of 346 tonnes of debris, and the pumping out of 64 million litres of water. This took 9 months and refurbishment costs of around $14m before some staff could move back into the office.

The catastrophe had a huge impact, as BP staff in Houston had to immediately work from home to keep the 'show on the road'. The BP philosophy in the USA on home working changed forever, as working from home became the new normal, and delivered results.

So, what will be different in the 'post-Coronavirus economy' (PCE)?

Some things may be rapidly accelerated by the Coronavirus pandemic, and others may well slow down. Here are some ideas, predictions and possible trends. They are to be treated with caution, but look to create some new thinking and shed light on what could happen:

Major changes – pre- and post-Coronavirus

Pre-Coronavirus Economy	Post-Coronavirus Economy
Mass international travel	More localised travel
Commuting	Working from home
Cheap flights	Scarce, expensive flights
Globalisation	Localisation
China dominant	'De-Chinafication'
London centric	Region centric
No borders in Europe	Tougher borders in Europe
Face-to-face socialisation	Virtual socialisation
Few international border restrictions	Some countries off limits to international travel for some time
Mass production in China and Far East	More local production
Just-in-time, high efficiency	Just in case, resilience, flexibility

Long, international supply chains	Shorter, local supply chains
Low unemployment, low inflation	High unemployment, inflation rising
Reasonable business cash flow	Zero or erratic cash flow, with huge credit crunch and high borrowings
No product or part shortages	Far East product shortages and availability
Cash is king	Cash is almighty
International mindset	National mindset

You may not agree with all these scenarios, but there is one thing we can be certain: the PCE will be very, very different, and the rules and practices of business will have to change substantially.

Taking advantage of the 'New Normal' in the PCE

How can new businesses take advantage? Here are some ideas:

- What parts of your business plan can be rethought and reconfigured to take account of the changes?
- How much can the business grow within its own organic cash flow?
- Brainstorm the opportunities for your new business in depth – how much nimbler and more flexible can you be, and how can you build it into your plan?
- Test your ideas and trial run your business from the kitchen table, garden shed or garage if possible
- Keep abreast daily of developments and major opportunities in your industry/sector
- Look at different ways of working or dealing with your customers

- Reinvent or restart your business proposition from scratch if you need to
- Establish ways your new business can be flexible to meet future challenges
- Follow the money

Chapter 50 Cash is no longer king – it is almighty

Entrepreneurs believe that profit is what matters most in a new enterprise. But profit is secondary. Cash flow matters most.

Peter Drucker – Management Guru, Educator and Author

Cash is no longer king – it is almighty

The Coronavirus has promoted cash from mere royalty (king) to a deity. In the PCE, cash is now almighty.

Less money will be available for start-ups, and many businesses and people will have extreme difficulty with their cash flows. Starting a business in the PCE will be much more challenging. As we have seen earlier, human ingenuity, however, has a wonderful way of overcoming huge obstacles, and many of these issues can be solved by innovation, new approaches, determination and skill.

We have said before there will be major opportunities available and there for the taking to those who are prepared and capable.

Coronavirus update – Fever Tree

At the time of writing, during the pandemic, Fever Tree (who we saw earlier in Chapter 25 as a great example of a disruptive business) declared their results. They reported *flat earnings, slow revenue growth and slightly reduced margins,* and also that Coronavirus was about to have a major impact. They are very well prepared, as they also reported a strong balance sheet, with no borrowings, and cash at year end of £128.3m.

Are there better examples out there of businesses being better prepared?

Starting a new Business in the PCE will be tough

Here are my initial ideas for a PCE business start-up checklist, which references back to the chapters in the book. This list has been prepared during the Coronavirus lockdown and may be amended and expanded in later editions.

Good luck – another opportunity like this may not come for another 50 to 100 years.

Post-Coronavirus business start-up checklist

Ref	Item	Chapter
1	Try to emulate the 'Holy Grail of start-ups'	Chapter 30 Page 139
2	Create a winning mindset, and build in resilience	Chapter 34 Chapter 48
3	Take great care and test your ideas carefully	Chapter 2 Chapter 16
4	Avoid giving any trade credit if possible – look for demand that is paid for by bank transfer, cash or card	Chapter 39
5	Be innovative	Chapter 10
6	Be decisive and act as fast as is reasonable	Chapter 9
7	Use the checklist and planning tools	Chapter 21
8	Customer due diligence: avoid buying or selling to failing or 'zombie' businesses	Chapter 16
9	Follow the money: self-funding may have to work – assume there will be little money from venture capitalists, banks or traditional new business sources. Do not wait too long	Chapter 39 Chapter 40 Chapter 50
10	Try family or relatives for funding – the older generation may still have some funds	Chapter 39
11	Try to work in parallel with the day job (if you have one) to minimise risk	Chapter 33

Secret No.50 With Coronavirus, cash has been promoted from 'king' to 'almighty'

Next Action: Ensure that your post-Coronavirus plan is about generating cash, cash and yet more cash. Be very conservative about spending cash in your business

Appendix 1 The '50 secrets of starting a business'

No	Secret	Next action
1	Cash is always king – no cash, no business	Read Chapter 39
2	Think clearly about your competitive advantage in your business plan	Include your competitive advantage in your business plan
3	After launch, there is little time to get a new business right before it potentially fails	Next Action: Read Chapter 33 and have a clear list of actions that can be achieved before launch
4	Address your business knowledge – eliminate the blind spot and learn what you don't know	Think about the limits of your knowledge, and look to improve in areas that need work
5	Do as much preparation, learning and understanding before launch as possible, to reduce risk	Build risk reduction into your plan and develop your ideas
6	Know your sector and geographical risks, and how they can be addressed	Look at the data for your sector and area, and note how those risks can be mitigated
7	Anyone can learn to be an entrepreneur, and run their own business providing they have the right personality traits	
8	Your business is like competing in the Heptathlon – prepare to succeed at all the events, not just the sprint	Establish which areas need work to achieve a good performance
9	Know your own skills, and find inventive ways of plugging skill gaps in your potential business	Establish key skills that need further work

10	Be solutions-driven to achieve success	Adopt a problem-solving approach: i.e. 'what are the solutions to this particular problem?'
11	Sensitivity to key timing points and the ability to respond are major ingredients of business success	Establish what your key timing points are likely to be
12	Self-reliance and the ability to bounce back from adversity are fundamental to business success	
13	Achieve a great lifestyle running a successful business	
14	Answer The Six Questions carefully	
15	Refine your business dream again and again to be a short, punchy and powerful statement	Write your dream down in one sentence
16	Carefully choose a business model that can be competitive in an era of enormous change and 'disruption'	Think about how your business idea can be strong, and disruptive if possible
17	Refine your search engine questions to sift and find the nuggets of knowledge that you really need amongst the huge volume of information	Try different approaches to your searches
18	Use Companies House to check up on your competition, customers and suppliers for free	Check out your biggest competitor on Companies House
19	Become a great researcher, and an expert on your business	Follow your market and future developments to help business success

20	'Jumping through the hoops' is a necessary part of starting a business. It shows commitment and staying power	Establish a plan on how to overcome your barriers one by one
21	Develop a positive approach to business ethics, as they become more important over time	State the ethical position of your business in one paragraph
22	A mentor will help – your business is much more likely to survive, and to succeed	Find a mentor through your contacts or local business support organisations
23	A written business plan, appropriate for the size and complexity of your start-up will provide external credibility and increase your knowledge of the business	Try drafting a business plan suitable for your type of start-up and get feedback
24	In the SWOT analysis, weaknesses and threats need to be covered comprehensively to avoid failure	Take time to consider your SWOT, and be brutally honest about weaknesses and threats
25	Engaging with the internet and social media is a great tool for building a successful business	Think about what digital presence is appropriate for your type of business, timescale, and how much it costs
26	The best start-up businesses minimise their commitment to premises, while maintaining a good location	Think how your business can provide a great product or service without committing to premises
27	If you have IP, formalise as much of your IP as you can to create an 'intangible asset' of value later on	List out your potential IP by category and take immediate steps to protect it

28	All businesses need a great team to succeed, even solo start-ups	Think carefully about what your team and advisers bring to the table, and their future potential
29	Clear contracts help all parties avoid disputes, protect IP and ensure commitment	Learn about contracts so you can use them for your new business' benefit
30	Think very carefully about the percentages of voting shares given to the founding team to avoid control problems later on	Learn about the different rights attaching to different percentages of shares in limited companies
31	Cash is king – it really is!	Prepare an accurate cash flow to make sure you generate the cash required to run the business
32	A conservative cash flow with known assumptions, and a contingency to cover 'unknown unknowns' makes sense	Plan your cashflow using a spreadsheet, but be very conservative
33	Know your business numbers, and where you can improve profitability without increasing your cost base	If volume is important, build a simple spreadsheet of the impact of volume sales on your business
34	Have as much of the set-up done as possible before you launch. This gives more time to grow the business at its most vulnerable stage	Prepare and complete your own set-up list before launch
35	Develop the winning mindset	Be positive about every setback and believe that it can be done. Find solutions
36	The right level of marketing activity will bring dividends	Do the sums for your planned marketing activity, working on conservative conversion rates

		to bring in the number of leads the business needs
37	Inventive indirect client approaches can be very productive	Think about new approaches you could make where you can add value to your business proposition
38	Consistent and regular marketing activity reduces stress	Make time for marketing activity, irrespective of how busy you are with delivery
39	Beware contacts selling, not buying	Review all prospects and close down those selling
40	Learn to negotiate the best deals you need to run the business well	Be very well prepared for every negotiation
41	Have at your fingertips, the right mobile systems that you need to run the business	Get comfortable with, and know your business numbers inside out
42	Your customers will love you lending them your money for 90 days if you let them	Find a way on payments to be a 'special case' and be paid early, or wait like the rest of the herd
43	Chase your debtors unmercifully all the time	Look to speed up cashflow with discounts or promotions. Be tough on customers that are bad payers
44	If you give credit, try to sell only to solvent customers that you have checked out	Run credit checks on all new customers and offer the right terms for a good credit rating. Cash in advance for poor quality customers allows you to sleep better at night
45	Use Nik Powell's mindset: be inventive and ruthless on negotiating and reducing costs	Think about clever ways you can set up the business with the lowest possible cost base. Always push the envelope to reduce costs
46	Entrepreneurs benefit by sharing and developing their knowledge within	Use a partner, friend or previous colleague as a sounding board

	networks to make up for their lack of infrastructure and support	
47	Everything can go wrong at any time, but if it does, it always means the cash flow is under pressure	Keep a 'rainy day' cash reserve if you can in the business and have a simple disaster plan. Use the 'war room' approach if required
48	There will be bumps in the road and major challenges for any business	Consider how resilient Walt Disney was to come back from bankruptcy and major adversity several times in order to achieve his dream
49	Stay on track by answering 'The ten key things to manage day-to-day'	What can I do differently to have a more successful and better business?
50	With Coronavirus, cash has been promoted from 'king' to 'almighty'	Ensure that your post-Coronavirus plan is about generating cash, cash and yet more cash. Be very conservative about spending cash in your business

Appendix 2 The 11-item post-Coronavirus business start-up checklist

Ref	Item	Chapter
1	Try to emulate the 'Holy Grail of start-ups'	Chapter 30 Page 139
2	Create a winning mindset, and build in resilience	Chapter 34 Chapter 48
3	Take great care and test your ideas carefully	Chapter 2 Chapter 16
4	Avoid giving any trade credit – if possible, look for demand paid for by bank transfer, cash or card	Chapter 39
5	Be innovative	Chapter 10
6	Be decisive and act as fast as is reasonable	Chapter 9
7	Use the checklist and planning tools	Chapter 21
8	Customer due diligence: avoid buying or selling to failing or 'zombie' businesses	Chapter 16
9	Follow the money: self-funding may have to work – assume there will be little money from venture capitalists, banks or traditional new business sources. Do not wait too long	Chapter 39 Chapter 40 Chapter 50
10	Try family or relatives for funding – the older generation may still have some funds	Chapter 39
11	Try to work in parallel with the day job (if you have one) to minimise risk	Chapter 33

Appendix 3: The 10 key things to manage day-to-day

1. Do I have enough cash to pay the salaries this month (and the PAYE and the VAT if applicable)?
2. Is there enough work for next month in my marketing funnel (and the three months after that)?
3. If there is not enough work, what can I do urgently to rectify the position?
4. Can I deliver all the work I have on time and at the right cost?
5. Is my pricing correct and will I make a profit on my current level of business?
6. Am I up to speed on my competitors' activities?
7. Can I look back in detail over the history of my business in my management reports?
8. What future developments are going to affect my market?
9. Am I totally up to date with tax, Companies House filings and administrative tasks?
10. What do I need to do differently today to have a more successful and better business tomorrow?

Appendix 4: The seven key skills

Key skills – the 'Heptathlon Challenge'

1. Motivation and mindset
2. Problem-solving skills
3. Ability to learn, understand and improve
4. Management skills
5. Customer-facing skills
6. Commercial skills
7. Administrative skills

Appendix 5: The 'Six Questions' that need to be clearly answered in the business plan

I keep six honest serving-men
(They taught me all I knew);
Their names are What and Why and When
And How and Where and Who.

Rudyard Kipling – Just So Stories 1902

Index

'Self-Starter' 40
10,000 Hours 22
100 Metre Hurdles 35
200 Metres 35
800 Metres 35
a dream 65
ability to 'finish' 39
Ability to learn 38, 243
accelerators 88, 89
Accounting 188
Administrative skills 38
Airbnb 68
Aldi 145
Allan Niblo 4
Amazon 68
Andrew Carnegie 149, 209
Angela Duckworth 158
Anita Roddick 32
Apollo 11 .... 9, 16, 103, 206
Apollo Programme 9, 20, 43, 93
Apple 32, 136, 212
Arthur Wellesley 72
Baker Ali 151, 154
Bank Manager 98
Banks 111, 176, 215, 218
barriers to entry 79, 80, 145

BBC TV 96
Bernie Sanders 67
Bill Gates 209
Biz Stone 46
blind spot 27, 235
Boris Johnson 115
BP 228, 229
Brainstorm 230
Brainstorming 104
Brand 20
bread 44, 144, 145, 153
Brexit 10, 155
Buckinghamshire Business First 4, 11, 88
Builder 59
Building Teams 57, 122
Business Competition 20
Business incubators 88, 89
Business Launch 156
Business Model 67, 68, 70
Business Model Canvas Template 96
Business Plan 18, 93, 94, 97, 122
Business Start-Up Failures 17
cash 16, 17, 18, 19, 47, 50, 53, 56, 75, 82, 83, 84, 93, 97, 122, 126, 135, 136, 137, 138, 139, 148, 154, 165, 166, 189, 190, 192, 193, 194, 195, 197, 198, 199, 200, 203, 207, 208, 212, 216, 217, 221, 230, 233, 235, 241, 242
Cash ... 17, 19, 56, 75, 83, 84, 93, 97, 135, 136, 189, 192, 230, 232, 235
Cashflow Model 137
Charles Darwin 16

Checkatrade 68, 100, 101, 107
Chess Masters 23
China 229
Chris the Plumber 197
Circle of Knowledge 26
COBRA Cobweb 73
COM 94, 95, 97
comfort zone 35, 47, 48
Commercial skills 38, 243
Commitment 40
Companies House 17, 74, 126
Company Birth and Death Rates 29
Competitive Advantage 20
Competitive Disadvantage 21
contract 52, 116, 128, 129, 130, 140, 145, 167, 192, 193, 196
Copyright 2, 115, 116
Coronavirus 9, 12, 106, 113, 159, 207, 214, 215, 216, 217, 219, 221, 222, 225, 229, 232, 233, 240, 241
Coronavirus COVID-19 .... 9, 214
Corporate social responsibility 86
Cost 20, 79, 150, 164
Costco 69, 70
COVID-19 207
CRM 164, 174, 177
culture 122, 159
Customer facing skills 38, 243
Customers' Needs 18
data 17, 31, 127, 155, 164, 187, 190, 235
Day rates 149

D-Day 225, 226, 227
De-Chinafication 229
Decisiveness 39
Department for Business, Energy and Industrial Strategy 14
Design Rights 115, 117
Dieselgate 86
differentiation 18, 101
Disney Company 209
Disneyland 209
Disruptive 68, 69
Disruptors 68, 197
Domino's Pizza 99
Donald Duck 209
Donald Rumsfeld 25
Dr Jon Wardle 4
Dragons 96, 98
Dunn & Bradstreet 198
Dyson 68
Early Stages 28
Economies of Scale 80
Egon Ronay 33
Entrepreneur 32, 33, 34, 35, 235
entrepreneurship 13, 32
Erica Ariel Fox 182
Erik Qualman 107
Ernst & Young 32, 33
Excel 136, 190
Experian 198
Facebook 78, 109, 205

failure rate ... 17, 30
Far East ... 220, 229, 230
FedEx ... 99
Fevertree ... 99, 100, 112, 113, 232
Financial Management ... 18
Flexibility ... 40
Follow the money ... 231, 233, 241
GDPR ... 170
Gene Kranz ... 16, 43, 93, 103, 120, 206
General Montgomery ... 225
George Shinn ... 204
Gig Economy ... 13
glass half empty ... 206
glass half full ... 206
Good judgement ... 39
Google ... 65, 179
Government ... 12, 79, 80, 106, 207, 214, 215, 217, 218, 219, 224
Greengrocers ... 222
Grit ... 158, 159
Hairdressing ... 190
Harold Macmillan ... 216
Harvard ... 143, 182
Harvey Mackay ... 182
Henry Ford ... 209
Heptathlon ... 35, 36, 37, 38, 40, 41, 48, 50, 57, 72, 235, 243
Heston Blumenthal ... 33
High Jump ... 35
HMRC ... 126, 156
Holy Grail ... 139

Howard Schultz........219
Hurricane Harvey........228
Hybrid business models........69
Ian Mackey........4, 224
Ice Cream........193, 198
Imperial War Museum........225
Inadequate Management........18
industry sector........14, 30
ING Bank........219
Insolvency........16
intermediaries........174
Internet........72, 107
Investopedia........67, 135, 144, 173
IP 115, 116, 118, 130, 131, 238
Jamie Oliver........100
Javelin........35, 36, 38
Jim Rohn........35
John Elkington........85
John F. Kennedy........64
Katarina Johnson-Thompson........36
Katharine Paine........143
Key Skills........38, 41, 243
key timing points........51, 52, 56, 236
kidology........103
Kingsmill........145, 146
KISS........188
kitchen table........112, 230
Knowings........72, 94
known knowns........25

known unknowns 25
KPMG 216
Lack of capital 18
Larry Page 209
launch 23, 24, 28, 29, 61, 97, 143, 157, 235
Le Manoir aux Quat' Saisons 33
Leadership failure 18
learning curve 9, 24, 179
Les Quat' Saisons 33
limited company 14, 74, 124, 125, 126, 132, 188
LinkedIn 78, 109, 170, 177, 178, 205
Location 18, 20, 30, 100, 101, 111
Logos 117
Long Jump 35
Malcolm Gladwell 22
Management Consultant 10, 59
Management Information 187, 188
Management skills 38, 243
Marco Pierre White 33
Mark Cliffe 219
Market Research 168
marketing 161, 163, 169, 174, 175, 176
Marketing 161, 163, 174, 176, 177, 178
marketing funnel 169, 170, 212, 242
Martin Luther King, Jr 225
McKinsey & Co 214
Mentoring 90, 91
Mentors 88
Michelin 33

Mickey Mouse 209, 210
Microsoft 136
Mindset 80, 158, 159, 225
Mission Statement 59, 62, 64, 65, 69
Monzo 68
Motivation 38, 243
MyBuilder 68, 100, 101, 107
Natalie Lisovskaya 37
National Film and Television School 4, 11
negotiate 53, 182, 183
Negotiating 53, 182, 183
Negotiation 182, 184
Netflix 68
network 54, 57, 60, 88, 89, 114, 168, 174, 175, 177, 205
New Normal 215, 230
Nigel Temple 108
Nik Powell 202, 204
Niklas Zennstrom 38
Numbers 136, 190
Obsolete 70
ONS 14, 17, 29, 30
Open-Minded 19
Opportunities 57, 103, 106, 221
P. J. O'Rourke 186
partner 19, 54, 120, 121, 202, 203, 204
Partnership 10, 125
Patents 79, 115, 118
PAYE 83, 84, 105, 124, 125, 155, 188, 196, 212, 242
PayPal 222

PCE 229, 230, 232, 233
Peter Drucker 232
Pimlico Plumbers 102
Plumber 59, 60, 62, 68, 70, 96, 100, 101, 107
Plumber Chris 62, 96, 100
Plumber Sam 60, 62, 68, 100
portfolio career 10, 13
Post Coronavirus Economy 229
Pragmatic 39
premises 112, 113, 197
President Kennedy 9, 64
Price 20, 146
Pricing 95, 100, 101, 143
Princes' Trust 11, 90, 190
Problem-solving 38, 243
Procurement 80
Product Knowledge 23
Prospects 177, 178, 179
publications 179
Randy Pausch 79
Ray Bradbury 154
Raymond Blanc 28, 33
Regina Brett 228
Reputation 20, 177
Research 72, 78, 147
Richard Branson 32, 100, 192, 202, 204, 209
risk register 224
Robert Frost 135
Rudyard Kipling 59, 244

S Truett Cathy 111
Saga 100
Sainsbury 145
sealed bid 148
Search Engines 73
Seasonality 165
Self -Reliance 54
self-employed 11, 14, 68, 116, 124, 125, 217
Self-Employment 10, 14, 124
Selling 161
Serendipity 168
Shot Put 35, 36, 37, 38
Six Questions 59, 72, 73, 94
skill gaps 42, 235
skills 38, 40, 42, 47, 48, 72, 103, 105, 112, 122, 183, 235, 243
Small Claims Court 200
SME's 14, 15
Social Media 78, 107, 109
Solo 120, 132
Solutions not Problems 27, 39, 43
sounding board 204
Spanish Flu 216
Special Resolution 132
Starbucks 65, 219
Status Quo 219
Steve Jobs 32, 209, 212
Strengths 103, 105
Summer Holiday 52
surveys 176

Survival of the Fittest 16
SWOT analysis 103, 104, 224, 237
team ... 9, 16, 18, 42, 45, 57, 93, 103, 105, 118, 120, 121, 122, 133, 206, 207
Teams 120
Tectonic Plate Shift 215
templates 97
Tenacity 39
Terms & Conditions 129
Tesco 44, 145
Tesla 69
The Knowings 40, 72
The Knowledge 22
Thomas Edison 209
Threats 103, 106
Time is of the Essence 24
Trade Credit 192, 193, 195
Trademarks 115, 117
traditional business model 68
Twitter 46, 65, 78, 109, 170, 177, 178
Ub Iwerks 210
Uber 68
Umbrella Companies 125
Umbrella Company 10
unknown unknowns 25
User experience 20
USP 99, 100, 101, 105
UX 108, 109
VAT 52, 83, 84, 105, 126, 155, 188, 192, 212, 242

Vertigo Films 4
Video Games 59
Virgin Records 202
VW 86
Waitrose 145, 146
Walmart 194, 195
Walt Disney 209
War Room 207
Warren Buffet 85
Weaknesses 103, 105
website 107, 108, 109, 115, 140, 177, 178, 179
Weight Watchers 100
Widgets 193
Wikipedia 43, 194, 216
winning mindset 158, 183, 233, 238, 241
Win-Win Deal 184
working capital 82, 84
World War I 210, 216
World War II 86, 216
Ziad K. Abdelnour 88
Zig Zigler 161
Zombie 216

www.ingramcontent.com/pod-product-compliance
Ingram Content Group UK Ltd.
Pitfield, Milton Keynes, MK11 3LW, UK
UKHW020132250726
13967UKWH00002B/601

9 781527 258136